HARMONY IN HUSTLE

YOGIC TOOLS TO DE-STRESS AND REJUVENATE

SANTHI CHEMUDUPATI

Disclaimer

The information presented in this book is intended for general knowledge and informational purposes only. It does not constitute medical advice. Readers should consult with a qualified healthcare professional before beginning any new exercise or wellness program. The author and publisher disclaim any liability for any injuries or damages that may result from the use of the information contained herein. Any names or characters, businesses or places, events or incidents, are fictitious. Any resemblance to actual persons, living or dead, or actual events is purely coincidental.

Preface

Dear Reader,
Warm greetings and deep gratitude for prioritizing your health.

As a yoga professional, I've witnessed firsthand students struggling with stress and seeking relief from its overwhelming grip. The pain of sleepless nights, digestive woes, and a general sense of dis-ease urged me to delve deeper into the root causes of stress. My MA dissertation research revealed similar struggles across all ages, inspiring me to find ways to support people in coping with life's challenges.

This book is the culmination of that desire. My goal is to bring a smile to those facing stress and help them connect with their inner guidance. I aim to provide effective coping mechanisms and tools for greater well-being.

"Harmony in Hustle: Yogic Tools to De-Stress and Rejuvenate" is my way of sharing inspiration, energy, and strength. It's a beacon of light to help the inner spark in every reader shine brightly, transforming stress into positive energy (eustress).

Welcome to this journey of discovering how to overcome stress with a smile! This book goes beyond simply understanding stress; it's about finding practical solutions that work for you, empowering you to tackle your own challenges with confidence using yogic principles all while having some fun.

But this book isn't just about empowerment; it's about connection. I've written it in a relatable and engaging way, so it feels like a conversation with a friend.

My goal is simple: to equip you with the tools, knowledge, and support you need to navigate life's challenges with resilience and grace. So, let's embark on this journey together, and may you find inspiration, empowerment, and perhaps even a few laughs along the way.

Love and Light,
Santhi

"The rhythm of the body,

The melody of the mind, and

The harmony of the soul creates

The symphony of life."

-B.K.S. Iyengar

CHAPTER 1

The Body Talks

Waking Up to Stress

Aanya, Rishi, and the City That Never Sleeps

The shrill ring of his phone at 4:30 AM was a cruel alarm clock for Rishi. It wasn't unusual for a jet-lagged call from a European distributor to kick start his day. By the time he reached the office, a lukewarm cup of coffee clutched in one hand and a tablet displaying financial reports in the other, the American workday was already in full swing. Between managing a global pharmaceutical company, navigating the ever-changing regulations of different countries, and placating a board with an insatiable appetite for growth, Rishi's days were a relentless dance across continents and time zones. Lunch was often a rushed affair at his desk, fueled by takeout and worry. The gym membership he religiously paid for collected dust, a silent reminder of the hobbies – rock climbing and photography – that were now distant memories. Evenings enjoyed playing video games, watching comedy shows or spent tinkering with his classic car are now a blur of paperwork , conference calls and presentations, the faces on his screen a kaleidoscope of nationalities. As exhaustion finally claimed him late at night, a singlc, nagging question echoed in his mind: was this relentless pursuit of success worth the sacrifice of everything that used to bring him joy? Little did he know, the answer was waiting to be unearthed within himself?

Rishi slammed his laptop shut, the screech of the hinges echoing the frustration building within him. He ran a hand through his already messy hair and let out a deep sigh.

Rishi: "Ugh, I can't take it anymore!" he muttered, burying his face in his hands.

 Meanwhile, across the world in bustling Mumbai, Aanya was grappling with her own version of a hectic life. Every morning, she braved the crowded local trains, crammed into compartments with hundreds of other commuters, all vying for a bit of space. The journey from her suburban home to her office in the heart of the city was a test of endurance and patience.

Aanya worked as a marketing manager for a fast-growing tech startup. Her days were filled with back-to-back meetings, tight deadlines, and a constant barrage of emails and messages. The pressure to deliver results was relentless, and the expectation to be available around the clock left her feeling perpetually on edge. The city's relentless pace only added to her stress. The honking of cars, the bustling crowds, and the constant noise created an environment where finding peace seemed impossible.

Lunch breaks were often skipped or spent at her desk, hurriedly eating a meal while reviewing reports. The evening commute back home was no less stressful. By the time she reached her apartment, she was too drained to engage in any of the activities she once enjoyed, like painting or reading. The weekends, meant for relaxation, were consumed by errands and catching up on work she couldn't finish during the week.

As she lay in bed at night, her mind raced with thoughts of unfinished tasks and upcoming projects. Sleep eluded her, replaced by a sense of anxiety that seemed to grow with each passing day. Aanya's health began to suffer – frequent headaches, a nagging backache from long hours at her desk, and a general sense of fatigue that never seemed to go away.

Aanya slammed her laptop shut, feeling the weight of her responsibilities pressing down on her.

I can't keep going like this," she whispered to herself. "What is this feeling that's choking me? Why can't I seem to catch my breath?"

Back there,

Unleashing the Power of Inner Wisdom

Rishi: I feel so overwhelmed. Like I'm drowning in deadlines, my phone won't stop buzzing, and my brain feels like mush. What is this feeling that's choking me? Why can't I seem to catch my breath?

A calm, yet clear voice resonated within Rishi. It felt like a wise and intuitive part of himself.

Inner Self: This feeling you have is stress, my friend. It's a natural reaction our body has to challenges and demands.

Rishi: A natural reaction? Stress? It feels more like a monster is gnawing at my insides. Why does it have to affect me so much?"

Inner Self: It can feel that way. Stress is like a signal from your body, telling you it's time to adapt. Remember that caveman facing a saber-toothed tiger? Because you are a sensitive being. You care deeply, and your body is trying to alert you to something that needs attention. It's a signal, a way to urge you to find a better balance.

Rishi: Balance? Right now, I feel like I'm on a tightrope, wobbling precariously. How can I find balance when everything feels like it's pulling me apart?

Inner Self: True balance isn't about a static state. It's about the ability to navigate the inevitable ups and downs of life. It's about having the strength to weather the storms and the flexibility to bend without breaking.

Rishi: But how do I get that strength and flexibility? How do I tame this stress monster?

 Inner Self: The answers lie within you, dear friend. Stress can arise from external pressures like deadlines, finances, or relationships. It can also be self-generated from worry, negative self-talk, or the feeling of being overwhelmed.

Rishi: Ugh, you're right on all counts. I keep replaying all the ways I could mess up, and it paralyzes me.

Inner Self: Those thoughts are like storm clouds obscuring the sunshine of your capabilities.

Remember, you've overcome challenges before. Didn't you? Trust yourself my friend!

Rishi: But how can I trust myself when I feel so out of control?

Inner Self: You have more control than you think. You control your focus, your attitude, and your actions. Forget not, you have the tools to manage stress, they may have gotten buried beneath the worry and anxiety. We can rediscover them together through practices that nurture your mind, body, and spirit and regain your inner peace.

Rishi: Practices? Like what?

Inner Self: What if there was a way to unwind, both physically and mentally, and find a sense of calm in the midst of the chaos? There are actually a number of techniques that can help you achieve this, and some people find that a practice that combines movement, breathing, and focused attention can be particularly effective.

Intrigued? It could be a way to release tension and find inner peace. Sounds interesting?

Rishi: Yes!

Inner Self: It is through yogic practices. Yoga is a powerful path to managing stress- a holistic approach, right way of living. It combines physical postures, breathing exercises, meditation, and mindfulness techniques by bringing about balance within the system. These practices can help you release tension, quiet your mind, and cultivate inner peace.

Rishi: Yoga? I don't know, I've always thought it was just for people who can bend themselves into pretzels.

Inner Self: Yoga is for everyone. It's a journey, not a destination. It's about finding what works for you, what brings you a sense of calm and centeredness.

Rishi: (A glimmer of hope appears in their eyes) Maybe you're right. Maybe it's worth a try. Where do I even begin?

Inner Self: We'll start slow and gentle. Each step you take toward managing your stress, towards finding your inner balance, is a step toward a more fulfilling and joyful life. This journey starts now. Are you ready?

Rishi: (Takes a deep breath) I am. Let's do this. But before we start, I'd really appreciate it if you could explain why my body reacts like this to challenging situations. This feeling of being overwhelmed is almost suffocating.

Inner Self: That's a great question. Imagine stress like stretching a muscle. If you push yourself too far, it gets tight and sore. That's what happens when your body is under stress for too long. It's a natural reaction designed to help you deal with challenges, but too much can be overwhelming.

Understanding the difference between stress, depression, and anxiety is important. Stress is that feeling of being overloaded, usually due to current demands. Depression is deeper and can linger for weeks or months. It's like getting stuck in a negative loop, dwelling on the past and feeling hopeless about the present. Anxiety, on the other hand, is about worrying excessively about the future. It can manifest as constant fretting about things that might not even happen, leading to unnecessary fear and tension.

Rishi: Wow that clarifies a lot. I sometimes feel all three at once! It's hard to tell which one is hitting me the hardest.

Inner Self: It's common to experience a mix of these emotions. But the good news is, by recognizing the signs, we can find ways to manage them all

Rishi: This feeling of stress is so overwhelming, but I don't even understand what's happening to me!

Inner Self: It's perfectly normal to feel confused. Stress is a complex reaction, but let's break it down. Imagine stress like a wave crashing on the shore. There are three main parts to understand:

1. **The Triggers** (Stressors): These are the things that cause the wave, like relationship troubles, work overload, or financial worries. Everyone reacts differently, so what stresses you out might not bother someone else. That's why it's important to track your stressors. Keep a journal and see what pops up most often.

2. **The Sensory Response**: Think of this like the water rushing towards the shore. When your body senses a stressor, it sends a signal through your nervous system, like an electric current traveling through wires. This is why you might feel a jolt of anxiety or a tightening in your chest. Stress makes these signals even faster and more intense.

3. **The Hormonal Reaction**: Now imagine the wave hitting the shore and causing a surge of power. Stress activates your glands, like the hypothalamus and adrenals, which release hormones like cortisol. These hormones give you a burst of energy to deal

with the stressor, but too much can have negative effects on your health.

Rishi: So, it's like a chain reaction? The stressor triggers a signal, which releases hormones that make me feel even worse?

Inner Self: Exactly. And there's one more piece to the puzzle: how stress can become a cycle. Think of the beach again. If the wave keeps crashing, the shore starts to erode. Similarly, chronic stress can damage your health.

Rishi: Wait, damage my health? How?

Inner Self: Stress can manifest in many ways. Physically, you might experience headaches, muscle tension, fatigue, or even digestive problems. Mentally, it can lead to anxiety, irritability, mood swings, and feelings of overwhelm or even depression. It can even affect your memory and concentration, making you more vulnerable to health problems, especially if you have weaker organs or systems in your body.

Rishi: Wow that sounds awful! Is there any way to tell if I'm stressed?

Inner Self: Absolutely! Stress often shows itself through various symptoms. If you're having trouble sleeping, changes in appetite, or find yourself using alcohol or tobacco more than usual, those could be signs of stress. Difficulty concentrating, memory problems, and racing thoughts are also common.

Rishi: This is all so much to take in. Is there anything I can do about it?

Inner Self: There's definitely hope! Understanding the different types of stress and their causes and symptoms is the first step. The good news is, there are many strategies to manage stress effectively, and some of the most powerful lie within you.

Rishi: Within me? What do you mean?

Inner Self: You have a natural capacity for healing and creating balance. Think about it - any disease, big or small, often originates in the mind. Stress, worry, and fear all take a toll on our well-being. That's where yoga comes in.

Rishi: That's amazing! So how exactly can yoga practices help heal these mind-body issues?

Inner Self: Chronic stress is a double whammy. The constant "fight or flight" response floods your system with hormones, which can lead to health problems down the line. Plus, when you're stressed, you often neglect your body's movement, which can create a vicious cycle of physical and emotional issues.

Think of your digestive system. It's sensitive to emotions, and stress can disrupt its smooth operation, leading to digestive woes. Ayurveda, an ancient Indian medical system, even suggests that low digestive fire is the root cause of many illnesses.
 Stress can definitely wreak havoc on your gut. When you're stressed, your digestion slows down, which can lead to a feeling of fullness, bloating, and even stomach aches. On the other hand, stress can also cause your large intestine to go into overdrive, leading to urgency and diarrhea.
 Yoga tackles both aspects of physical and emotional wellbeing. By combining physical postures, breathing exercises, gentle stretching, relaxation and meditation, these not only improves flexibility but also calms the nervous system, utilizes the energy ideally maintaining hormonal balance and leading to a more peaceful state of mind.
 It thus helps manage stress hormones, improves circulation, and promotes better digestion – all contributing to a healthier, more balanced you.
Yoga is a holistic practice that works on both the body and mind.
Rishi: So, you're saying a relaxed mind can actually improve my health?

Inner Self: Absolutely! Our body's functions are controlled by a complex interplay of hormones and chemicals. Stress disrupts this delicate balance, sending chaotic signals from the mind to the brain and glands. This can lead to a domino effect, with one issue triggering another, eventually manifesting as physical problems like high blood pressure or heart disease.

Rishi: Wait, are you saying stress can cause all sorts of different diseases?

Inner Self: Recent studies suggest that conditions like hypertension, diabetes, and even heart problems might not be entirely separate diseases. They could all be part of one larger syndrome with a common root cause: a stressed mind. Yoga, by promoting relaxation and inner peace, can address this root cause and help prevent these conditions from developing.

Rishi: Wow, that's incredibly insightful! Yoga never seemed like more than physical poses before, but the idea of working on both my mind and body to manage stress feels truly holistic. This could be the turning point I've been searching for. Tell me more, Inner Self. Why is it that some people seem to crumble under pressure while others seem to thrive?

How can yoga help navigate those individual differences?

Inner Self: (Smiling) I knew you'd be interested! The beauty of yoga is that it's adaptable to everyone. Think about it this way, imagine everyone has a different type of stress response. Some people get jittery and anxious, their minds racing a mile a minute. Others bottle things up, feeling tense and tight in their bodies.

Rishi: That makes sense. So, is there a different type of yoga for each person?

Inner Self: The beauty of yoga is its versatility. A workshop like the one happening this weekend, for example, can be a great way to explore different practices and see if it resonates with you. Some techniques, like gentle stretches and deep breathing exercises, can be calming for an overactive mind. Other postures, held for longer periods, can help release tension and promote relaxation in a stressed body. And the therapist will guide you for the suitable practices further.

Rishi: A workshop, huh? Interesting. Would it be intimidating for a beginner like me?

Inner Self: Not at all! Most workshops cater to beginners, and they're a fantastic way to learn proper techniques and find a practice that works for you specifically. You might even meet some friendly people along the way who are also on their own yoga journeys.

(Suddenly, Rishi's gaze falls on a small palm-sized booklet lying forgotten on the corner of his desk. He vaguely remembers seeing it earlier that day.)

A Journey Begins

Rishi: Wait a minute... where did this come from?

Inner Self: (Chuckles softly) you picked it up at the community center this morning. Remember, the one about "stress management through yoga?"

Rishi: (Recognition dawns on his face) Oh yeah... right. I meant to take a look at it later, but things got hectic...

Inner Self: See, this is exactly what I'm talking about! You're so focused on the external demands that you neglect your inner well-being. Maybe it's time you took a step back and explored what this booklet has to offer.

Rishi: (Hesitates, then picks up the booklet) De-Stress & Rejuvenate: A 3-Day Yoga & Mindfulness Workshop... hmm... that actually sounds pretty good right now.

Inner Self: (With a hint of encouragement) it could be the turning point you need, Rishi. Give it a try.

(Rishi flips through the booklet, reading about the workshop's content and benefits. A flicker of hope ignites in his tired eyes.)

Rishi: (To himself) maybe... maybe you're right. Three days can't hurt, can they?

(He pulls out his phone and starts searching for the workshop registration details.)

Rishi sits down at his computer, a spark of hope igniting within him. He searches online and finds the website promoting the "De-Stress & Rejuvenate" workshop. After browsing the details, he clicks the "Register Now" button with a newfound determination.)

Rishi: Done. Looks like I'm going to give this yoga thing a shot. Thanks...inner self.

(The inner self beams, its form shimmering brighter for a moment.)

Inner Self: A wise decision, Rishi.

Inner Self: (With satisfaction) now that's the Rishi I know. The one who's willing to take a step towards a healthier, happier life.

(Rishi smiles faintly, a glimmer of determination replacing the stress lines on his face.)

Rishi: (Grins) maybe that's not such a bad idea after all. Thanks... for the nudge, me.

Inner Rishi: (Smiles warmly) Always here for you, Rishi. Now, shall we finish clearing this desk? A less cluttered workspace can work wonders for the mind. (Rishi laughs, the tension easing from his shoulders. He and his inner self begin tackling the mess together, a newfound resolution flickering in Rishi's eyes.)

CHAPTER 2

Unrolling the Mat: Unveiling the Power Within

(Sunlight streams through the yoga studio windows. Upbeat instrumental music plays softly in the background, as students begin to arrive, unrolling mats and chatting excitedly.)

Yoga Therapist: (Beaming) Welcome everyone! So happy to see all your bright faces this morning. For those of you who haven't met me, I'm Yogi Seshi Priya, your yoga therapist for the next few days. I've been practicing yoga since childhood, and the past seven years I've been dedicated to helping people like you integrate this ancient practice into their modern lives.

(Raises an eyebrow with a playful grin)

Because let's face it, who couldn't use a little more Zen in this crazy world, right?

(Laughter ripples through the room)

But seriously, my mission is to contribute to a world where everyone, yes, even the busiest bees among us, can find joy and well-being through movement.

(Looks around the room, encouraging introductions)

So, to get to know each other a bit better, why don't we all go around and introduce ourselves? Maybe tell us your name, what you do for a living, and most importantly, what brought you to this amazing yoga mat today, and maybe, just maybe, a tiny stressor that's been bugging you lately. Consider it a stress confession booth, completely judgment-free!

(Points to a young woman with a bright smile) Alright, sunshine, why don't you start us off?

Student 1: Hi there! I'm Sarah, a graphic designer. Deadlines are definitely my stress monster, especially with this new project. But I also haven't slept well this week, which isn't helping the creativity flow.

Yogi Seshi: (Nods sympathetically) Ah, the designer's dilemma! Deadlines and sleep deprivation - a classic combo. (Turns to a man in a suit, tapping his pen rhythmically) Your turn, sir!

Student 2: Mark, software engineer here. Feeling pretty burnt out lately. Work is demanding, and by the time I get home, the last thing I want to do is hit the gym. But I know I need to move more.

Yogi Seshi: (Chuckles) I hear you, Mark. The post-work slump is real! (Gestures to a man with a relaxed posture) And friend you in the cozy corner, what's your story?

Student 2: Sounds fun! I'm David, a graphic designer by day and a chronic neck-tense sufferer by night. I Hope yoga can help with that.

Yogi Seshi: Welcome, David! Neck tension is a common complaint these days. Yoga can definitely be your knight in shining armor (or should I say, gomukhasana?) for that.

Student 3: It's Olivia. I'm a teacher, and let me tell you, wrangling little humans can be stressful! Plus, grading papers late at night isn't exactly a recipe for Zen.

Yogi Seshi: (Laughs) Olivia, you're preaching to the choir! Teachers deserve a standing ovation for all they do. (Looks at the group)

 Alright everyone, it seems we've got a great crew here – designers, teachers, accountants – all united by the desire to ditch some stress and embrace a healthier lifestyle.

Over the next three days, that's exactly what we'll be doing! We'll explore THE YOGIC TOOL KIT; ancient yogic practices passed down through generations, breathing techniques to calm the mind, and gentle postures that will leave you feeling stronger, more flexible, and yes, definitely less stressed.

(Raises her finger mischievously)

And yes, there will be some breathing exercises (pranayama) too. No, don't worry, it's not like hyperventilating in a paper bag! Think of it as internal bubble wrap – popping away all that pent-up stress.

(More laughter)

Yogi Seshi: Welcome everyone! Let's dispel the myth that yoga is just about fancy poses and deep breaths. It's a philosophy, a way of life designed to cultivate balance and well-being. Today, we'll explore ancient yogic wisdom that's surprisingly relevant to our modern struggles.

(Looks around the room with a twinkle in her eye)

Buckle up! By the end of this workshop, I want to show you how incorporating simple yogic practices into your daily routine can revolutionize your health and happiness. No pretzel poses required, just a willingness to move, breathe, and rediscover joy.

Ready to tame those inner stress monsters and build a balanced life?

(A chorus of enthusiastic "Yesses!" fills the room)

Yogi Seshi: Fantastic! But first, a disclaimer: there will be no pretzel poses. This is your journey, tailored to your needs. (Grins) Now, let's loosen up with gentle stretches and a calming breathing technique. Imagine yourself like a calm lake reflecting the sky, feeling as light and relaxed as a feather floating on a gentle breeze or sinking into a cloud of pure comfort, that's the level of relaxation we're aiming for! Ready?

Shifting Gears: Understanding Stress

Before we dive into yoga, let's understand how our bodies react to challenges. Imagine encountering a bear in the forest! Our body naturally goes into "fight-or-flight" mode, a stress response mediated by the nervous system, hormones, and immune system. Our heart rate increases, adrenaline pumps, and muscles tense – all to prepare us to either fight the bear (fight) or run away (flight). This stress response is essential for our survival in the face of danger.

However, in our modern world, the "bears" we face are often deadlines, traffic jams, or demanding relationships. These chronic stressors keep our alarm system blaring constantly. This chronic stress can be incredibly harmful, leading to anxiety, depression, and even physical health problems.

But there's good news! Not all stress is bad. Positive stressors, called eustress, can actually be motivating and energizing. Think of the excitement of a new project or the challenge of a yoga pose you're trying to master. Eustress can help us grow and improve.

 So, as you can see, stress can be a real double-edged sword. It can help us survive a bear attack, but it wreaks havoc on our health if it sticks around too long. The key to a healthy life lies in finding a balance between these two types of stress. But fear not! There's a powerful antidote to chronic stress, and it's been around for thousands of years. Yoga!

It's a holistic approach to living a balanced and healthy life.

Yogi Seshi: Let me share some of the basic principles of yoga practice. During this 3 day workshop we shall concentrate on these three main areas:

- Asana (Postures): These physical postures improve flexibility, strength, and body awareness.

- Pranayama (Breathing Techniques): Controlled breathing techniques calm the mind and regulate the nervous system.

- Meditation: Practices that cultivate focus, inner peace, and self-awareness.

Lesson Plan and Essential Reminders:

Our journey begins with a warm-up through Sukshma Vyayam (gentle exercises) to prepare your body for the practice. We'll then move into relaxing stretches followed by twisting and restorative asana's (postures) to improve flexibility and release tension. Finally, we'll conclude with Shavasana (Corpse Pose), a deep relaxation practice. But firstly, the essentials.

- Coordinate movement with breath: Breathe deeply and naturally throughout the practice.

- Empty stomach or 3-hour gap after meals: This allows for optimal digestion and practice comfort.

- Well-ventilated room: Always ensure adequate air circulation for a comfortable practice.

- Comfortable clothing: Wear loose-fitting clothing that allows for free movement.

- Sunlight: If available, practice in natural soothing morning light for added benefits.

- Posture: Maintain good alignment throughout the practice, but don't push yourself beyond your limits.

- Awareness: Pay attention to your body's sensations and signals. Don't force anything.

- The most important reminder is to always be aware of the indications, contraindications, and benefits of any yoga posture (asana), as such any yogic practice, and follow the right process as guided by a trained yoga teacher.

Embrace the journey, and let's begin! Yogi Seshi started the session.

As Yogi Seshi led the group through gentle warm-up exercises, a sense of camaraderie bloomed among the participants, most of them yoga newbies like Rishi. A young woman named Sarah, her ponytail bouncing with each movement, accidentally touched her toes while trying a standing forward fold.

Sarah (laughing): Oops! Guess I'm more flexible than I thought!

A ripple of laughter filled the room, even Yogi Seshi chuckled, his eyes crinkling at the corners.

Yogi Seshi: Flexibility comes in all shapes and sizes, Sarah. It's not about how far you can bend, but how comfortable you feel in the pose.

Next, they moved on to Marjari asana (Cat-Cow Pose). A man in the back, let's call him David, arched his back a little too enthusiastically during the "cow" pose, resembling a startled cat more than a relaxed one.

David (sheepish grin): Maybe I should stick to cat for now.

The group erupted in good-natured laughter, easing any initial self-consciousness. Yogi Seshi offered a playful nudge.

Yogi Seshi: No worries, David. We all start somewhere. Think of the cow as a gentle arch, not a full-on backbend.

During Veerabhadra asana (Warrior II Pose), a woman named Maria struggled to balance, her arms wobbling like a sailboat in a storm. Sensing her frustration, Rishi, who found the pose surprisingly comfortable, offered a reassuring smile.

Rishi: Hey, it happens to the best of us! Just find your center of gravity and take it slow.

Maria returned a grateful smile and took a deep breath, finding her footing with renewed focus.

As they transitioned into Downward-Facing Dog, a pose known for its inversion, Sarah let out a surprised giggle.

Sarah: Whoa, the world looks different upside down!

Yogi Seshi (chuckling): It does, doesn't it? Take a few breaths here, Sarah. Let gravity do its work and lengthen your spine.

Throughout the practice, Yogi Seshi's gentle guidance and encouraging words fostered a lighthearted atmosphere. He even incorporated some playful modifications for beginners, like suggesting holding onto a chair for balance in Veerabhadra asana (Warrior III Pose). By the end of the session, the initial awkwardness had melted away, replaced by a sense of accomplishment and shared laughter.

Rishi (smiling): Wow, I actually did all those poses! Never thought I'd be able to do that.

Sarah (nodding): Me neither! And it wasn't even that hard, thanks to Yogi Seshi's funny stories. Finally relaxation time!

Day One Winds Down

As the final sunbeam faded from the studio window, Yogi Seshi guided the group through a deeply relaxing Shavasana (Corpse Pose). Gentle breaths filled the room, and a sense of peaceful stillness descended. After a few moments of quiet contemplation, Yogi Seshi's voice broke the silence.

Yogi Seshi: Thank you all for joining me on this journey today. Remember, yoga is a practice, not a destination. Take these tools with you, and explore them further at home.

Yogi Seshi chimed in, a warm smile on her face. "I have shared a simple deep breathing exercise with you all. Tonight, before drifting off to sleep, find a quiet corner and practice. There's also a guided relaxation audio I've shared. Feel free to use it to deepen your experience."

The camaraderie forged during the session hinted at the supportive community Rishi might find as he continued his yoga journey. As they filed out of the studio, there was a lightness in their steps and a spark of hope in their eyes, ready to face their inner stress monsters with newfound tools and a dash of laughter.

Homeward Bound: A Spark of Hope

The fluorescent lights of the elevator flickered as it lurched to a stop on Rishi's floor. Stepping out, he was greeted by the familiar dimness of his apartment hallway. The city's ceaseless hum faded into a muffled drone as he shut the door behind him, the weight of the day finally pressing down.

Exhaustion clung to him like a second skin. The endless emails, the pressure-filled conference calls, the gnawing feeling of being pulled in a dozen directions – it all swirled in his head. Yet, beneath the fatigue, a strange sense of invigoration pulsed. Memories of the day's workshop flickered in his mind – the insightful discussions that challenged his perspective, the surprisingly gentle stretches that coaxed tightness from his muscles, and the profound sense of calm he'd experienced during Shavasana, lying there like a grounded mountain amidst the storm.

It felt like a seed of hope, a tiny spark nestled in the fertile soil of his discontent. Maybe, just maybe, there was another way. Perhaps this yoga journey, a path he'd stumbled upon almost by accident, could offer him the tools to navigate the chaos without sacrificing himself completely. With a sigh that carried both weariness and a flicker of excitement, Rishi kicked off his shoes and got ready. Stepping out of the warm shower, Rishi felt a layer of tension peel away. He wrapped himself in a soft towel, a sense of curiosity battling the exhaustion in his muscles. Rishi changed into comfortable clothes and headed towards the living room.

Following Yogi Seshi's advice, he found a quiet spot on his living room floor. He closed his eyes, focusing on his breath. Inhaling slowly through his nose, he felt a cool sensation fill his chest. As he exhaled through his mouth, tension seemed to leave his body with each exhale.

After a few cycles of deep breathing, Rishi put on the guided relaxation audio. A gentle voice soothed him, guiding his attention to different parts of his body, releasing any remaining tension. With each instruction, Rishi felt himself sinking deeper into relaxation.

Reflections in the Stillness

As the audio concluded, Rishi lay still on the floor, bathed in the soft glow of the bedside lamp. The worries of the day seemed distant, replaced by a newfound sense of calmness. He replayed the day's lessons in his mind, particularly the concept of stress as a double-edged sword. Perhaps, he thought, the key wasn't eliminating stress altogether but learning to manage it effectively.

A flicker of hope sparked within him. Maybe, just maybe, there was a way to navigate the demands of his life without sacrificing his well-being. With a deep breath and a newfound sense of resolve, Rishi closed his eyes, ready to drift off to a sleep filled with the promise of a more balanced future. The journey to tame his inner stress monsters had just begun.

(As Rishi lies on his bed, eyes closed, reflecting on the day)

Rishi: Wow, that was...unexpected. Yoga always seemed so intimidating, but Yogi Seshi made it so much fun!

Inner Self: (Soft, calming voice) See? I told you it wouldn't be all pretzel poses and chanting.

Rishi: (Chuckles) Right, right. Though, I have to admit, downward-facing dog did feel a little more like downward-facing disaster.

Inner Self: (Laughter) Hey, everyone starts somewhere! But seriously, didn't you feel a difference after those stretches and breathing exercises? Like a knot in your shoulders you didn't even know was there just...untied itself?

Rishi: You know what? I think you're right! And that whole thing about stress being like a fire...that made so much sense. I spend all day running around, putting out little fires at work, and no wonder I feel so drained!

Inner Self: Exactly. But wait, there's more to yoga than just stress relief, you know.

Rishi: That's what I was wondering! Yogi Seshi mentioned this yogic philosophy...something about ancient wisdom? What's that all about?

Inner Self: Well, it's not just about the physical postures (asana). Yoga is a whole way of life, a system that's been around for thousands of years. It teaches things like self-discipline, mindfulness, a stavik diet, and living a balanced life.

Rishi: Balance? That's definitely something I need! Remember when Seshi joked about stress not discriminating? She had a point. She looked at me and said something about chasing deadlines across continents...definitely hit a nerve there.

Inner Self: (Laughter) See? Yoga philosophy can be very practical. It offers ways to manage stress, improve focus, and even increase your energy levels, no matter your profession.

Rishi: That teacher analogy cracked me up too! "Think of yoga as a toolbox..." I like that. Maybe with the right tools, I can finally build a better fire pit, not a raging inferno.

Inner Self: Bingo! The next two days, you will then delve deeper into this yogic toolbox. Get ready for more fun, more exploration, and maybe even a few more laughs along the way.

Rishi: Sounds good to me. I'm starting to see how yoga can be more than just exercise. It could be a key to unlocking a whole new way of living.

Inner Self: Now that's the spirit! Remember, it's a journey, not a destination. So, relax, breathe, and get ready for day two. You might surprise yourself at what you discover.

(Rishi takes a deep breath, a small smile playing on his lips. He drifts off to sleep, a spark of newfound curiosity about yoga and its philosophy flickering within.)

CHAPTER 3

Toolbox Time

Day 2 of workshop: Deepening the Practice

(Yogi Seshi walks into the room with a mischievous grin, holding a basket overflowing with colorful scarves and blindfolds.)

Welcome Back, Seekers of Balance!

Yogi Seshi: Namaste everyone, and welcome to Day Two of your yoga journey! Did you all manage to tame those inner stress monsters after yesterday's session?

(Chuckles)

But seriously, today's all about exploring the deeper side of yoga – the philosophy and wisdom that's been guiding yogis for millennia. To begin, we'll embark on a guided visualization, a practice that harnesses the power of imagination. Imagine visualization as a tool to help us cultivate the feelings that empower us, the ones that bring us joy and resilience, and gently release those that hold us back. It's a skill that can bring a sense of calm even amidst the chaos of daily life. Through visualization, we can tap into our inner strengths and envision the goals we want to achieve, making them feel more real and attainable.

As we delve deeper, we'll also explore the fascinating interplay between our mind and body. We'll discuss the physiological changes that occur within us during stress, understanding how it impacts everything from our blood pressure to our digestion. This knowledge empowers us to manage stress more effectively.

Finally, to integrate what we've learned, we'll flow through a sequence of gentle stretches, breathing exercises, and a deeply relaxing practice. I call it PACE - Postures, Awareness, Centering, and Expansion - designed to help us cultivate those wonderful feel-good hormones: Dopamine, Oxytocin, Serotonin, and Endorphins, all fostered by yoga. So, get comfortable on your mats, open your minds, and let's PACE into action!

Are you ready with your mind, body and being to begin crafting a toolbox for a more balanced and joyful life!

Yes!!! Echoed

(Raises the basket with a flourish)

Don't worry, no need to wear your fanciest yoga pants for this one! Grab a scarf and a blindfold, and find a comfortable spot on your mat. Close your eyes, and take a few deep breaths.

(Walks around the room, gently placing scarves and blindfolds within reach)

Now, imagine yourselves standing at the edge of a bustling marketplace. Sounds and smells bombard your senses - the rhythmic chatter of vendors, the tempting aroma of spices, and the cacophony of traffic. You feel the stress of the crowd begin to tighten your shoulders, quicken your breath.

(Pauses for a beat)

Suddenly, a narrow alleyway catches your eye. Intrigued, you step off the main road and into the cool, quiet darkness. The sounds of the marketplace fade away, replaced by the gentle chirping of birds and the rustling of leaves.

(Waves her hand as if parting a curtain)

Here, in this hidden oasis, you find a serene garden. Sunlight filters through the leaves, dappling the ground with light and shadow. The scent of fresh flowers fills the air. The sound of chirping birds, the sight of colorful butterflies, and the soft blossoms of lotuses are a treat to the senses. Take a moment to truly feel the peace of this place. (Quietly)

Let go of any tension you were carrying from the marketplace. Feel your shoulders soften, your breath slow and deepen. This, my friends, is the power of your imagination. You have the ability to find this peaceful sanctuary within yourself, no matter where you are in the external world.

(Raises her voice slightly)

Now, gently remove your blindfolds. The marketplace may still be there, but you carry this sense of calm within you. This is the essence of yoga philosophy – cultivating inner peace even amidst life's challenges. (Smiles warmly)

So, are you ready to explore how yoga can help you create your own inner sanctuary, even in the midst of everyday chaos?

BODY VILLE

Now let's understand the physiological changes in the body during stress

Imagine your body as a bustling city, with every part playing a crucial role. But what happens when stress hits? It's like a city-wide emergency! Today, we're diving into a fun and informative video that explores the fascinating world of stress and its impact on your "Body Ville." Get ready to meet the Inner crew – your brain, hormones, organs – and witness the internal chaos that unfolds when you're feeling overwhelmed. By the end of the session, you'll not only understand the science behind stress, but also discover practical ways to restore peace and harmony to your inner city!

Let's take a look!

(Fade into a bustling city scene. Cars honk, people rush by, construction clangs. A stressed-out looking young person, Sam, walks through the crowd, overwhelmed.)

Narrator: Ah, City Ville! A place where dreams are chased and deadlines are met... with a side of major stress! But what's happening inside Sam when they feel overwhelmed? Let's take a trip to Body Ville!

(The scene shifts to a brightly colored cartoon city. A tiny house labeled "Brain" sits at the center. Next to it is a grand building labeled "Adrenal Glands".)

Narrator: In the bustling command center, the Brain, a tiny mayor in a spiffy suit, receives a message. It's a flashing red alert!

Brain (frantic): Stress alert! Everyone to their battle stations!

(Two excitable city workers, Cortisol and Adrenaline, burst out of the Adrenal Glands building.)

Cortisol and Adrenaline (in unison): Fight or flight! Fight or flight!

Narrator: Our trusty emergency crew, Cortisol and Adrenaline, race into action!

(Cortisol zooms towards a muscular building labeled "Muscles" and starts pumping them up with inflatable weights.)

Cortisol: Bulk up, muscles! We got to be ready for anything!

Muscles (grunting): Feeling pumped! Ready to fight this stress monster!

(Adrenaline zooms to the heart-shaped building labeled "Heart" and starts cranking a giant dial.)

Adrenaline: Heart, beat faster! We need to get all this energy flowing!

Heart (pounding): Lub-dub, lub-dub, lub-DUB! Faster, faster!

Narrator: Meanwhile, down on Lungs Lane, Lungs are working overtime.

Lungs (puffing): Deep breaths, everyone! Got to get that oxygen pumping!

Narrator: But in the belly of the beast, the Stomach, things are getting a little wonky.

Stomach (groaning): Ugh, I don't know what to do! Should I digest lunch or hold off? These signals are all messed up!

(The Stomach twists and turns in confusion.)

Narrator: Upstairs in the Sleep Apartments, things aren't much better.

Brain (whispering to Sleep): Shhh, we can't sleep yet! There's danger!

Sleep (yawning): But... but its cozy time...

Narrator: Over in the Memory Lane neighborhood, things are foggy.

Brain (scratching its head): Huh? Where did I put those keys again?

Narrator: And over at the Mood Boulevard, things are taking a turn for the worse.

Neurotransmitters (crying): Wah! The balance is off! We're sending mixed signals!

Narrator: Sam feels the effects all over Body Ville. Tight muscles, a churning stomach, racing thoughts, and a grumpy mood. Yikes!

(Sam appears above Body Ville, looking even more stressed.)

Narrator: But wait, there's hope! By understanding how stress affects Body Ville, Sam can learn to manage it. Yoga, deep breathing, and healthy habits can help activate the relaxation response and bring peace back to Body Ville.

Brain (calmer): Okay team, stand down! False alarm. Let's get back to normal operations.

Body Ville Inner crew (all sighing in relief): Phew! That was close.

Narrator: Remember, Sam, listen to your body's messages. Take a deep breath, find healthy ways to manage stress, and your Body Ville will be a happy and healthy place to live!

(The scene fades out with a peaceful view of Body Ville.)

So, what did you all think of Bayville's adventure? Did the video help shed light on how stress affects your body in a relatable way? Now that you understand the internal communication, we can delve deeper into practical tools and techniques to manage stress effectively and create a calmer, more resilient Body Ville!

(The video ends, showing a peaceful Body Ville. The yoga therapist smiles at the students.)

Yogi Seshi: So, what did you all think of our trip to Body Ville?

Maya (enthusiastically): Wow that was amazing! I never realized how much goes on inside our bodies when we're stressed. It's like a whole internal drama plays out!

David (chuckling): Right? My stomach was definitely the most dramatic Rishi in my Body Ville. All that churning and growling whenever I had a deadline.

Rahul: Me too! And the whole fight-or-flight thing... explains why I freeze up during presentations instead of running away screaming.

Alex: (Raises an eyebrow) Running away from presentations might be a better option, Rahul.

(Everyone laughs)

Raj (thoughtfully): It was really helpful to see the "fight or flight" response explained like that. I always thought stress was just feeling overwhelmed, but now I understand the physical side of it. The racing heart, the tight muscles... it makes sense why I get headaches so often when I'm stressed.

Yogi Seshi: Absolutely, Raj. Stress hormones like cortisol and adrenaline are incredibly powerful. They're designed to help us deal with short-term threats, but when they're released chronically, they can wreak havoc on our bodies.

Maya: Chronic stress? You mean like, if you're always feeling stressed, not just in emergencies? Seriously though, understanding this whole stress response makes me wonder... are we just doomed to be these cortisol-pumping machines every day.

Yogi Seshi: Exactly, Maya. Think about it like this. Imagine your body is a well-oiled machine, with every part working in harmony. When you're stressed, it's like hitting the gas pedal on that machine. Everything speeds up, your heart pumps faster, your blood pressure rises, your digestion slows down. In the short term, it can be helpful. But if you keep your foot on the gas all the time, eventually the machine starts to break down.

David: That's scary! So, what kind of long term effects can constant stress have?

Yogi Seshi: It's a long list, unfortunately. (Chronic stress can weaken your immune system, making you more susceptible to illness. It can increase your risk of heart disease, high blood pressure, and even diabetes. It can also lead to anxiety, depression, and sleep problems.)

(Points to a chart on the board)

Chronic stress, with its constant release of cortisol and adrenaline, can have a significant impact on our health.

This chart shows some of the potential consequences of chronic stress:

Weakened immune system: Stress hormones can suppress the immune system, making you more susceptible to illness.

High blood pressure: The fight-or-flight response causes a temporary increase in blood pressure. Chronic stress can keep your blood pressure elevated, increasing the risk of heart disease and stroke.

Digestive problems: Stress can disrupt the digestive system, leading to problems like heartburn, constipation, and diarrhea.

Weight gain: Cortisol can increase your appetite and cravings for sugary and fatty foods. It can also promote fat storage, particularly around the abdomen.

To deepen your understanding of your body's stress response, I encourage you to take some time for a personal body scan at home. Notice where you hold tension and explore ways to release it. We'll have a chance to share our findings and support each other at the end of the workshop.

The Lifestyle Connection

Many of you, I'm sure, can relate to feeling overwhelmed by stress. Headaches, tight muscles, trouble sleeping - they all become unwanted companions. But what if I told you a lot of these issues are directly linked to our daily habits?

David: Interesting! So you're saying stress isn't just some external monster attacking us?

Yogi Seshi: Exactly! Think of stress as a fire. We all experience sparks throughout the day, but how big the fire gets depends on the kind of fuel we throw on it. Our lifestyle choices - diet, sleep, activity levels - all play a major role.

Sara: Like pouring gasoline on the flames with unhealthy eating and late nights?

Yogi Seshi (Smiling): Precisely! Doctors often call these issues "lifestyle disorders" because they're heavily influenced by our daily routines. Conditions like hypertension (high blood pressure) and chronic stress can often be traced back to these habits.

Praveen: Wow, that's a powerful statement. So, what can we do to prevent the fire from getting out of control?

Yogi Seshi: Fantastic question! This is where yoga steps in beautifully. Think of yoga as a multi-tool for building a healthier lifestyle.

As we move through postures (asana), we not only strengthen and tone our bodies, but we also calm the nervous system.

David: Wait, so yoga can actually help lower stress and blood pressure?

Yogi Seshi: Absolutely! Studies have shown regular yoga practice can significantly reduce stress hormones like cortisol and lower blood pressure.

Sara: That's amazing! But what about the other aspects of lifestyle?

Yogi Seshi: Great point! Yoga encourages a holistic approach. Many yogis follow principles of Yama & Niyama, which are ethical guidelines for living a balanced and meaningful life. Also, getting enough sleep, eating nourishing foods, and cultivating a sense of moderation.

Remember, yoga isn't just about fancy poses on a mat. It's about creating a toolbox of practices and principles that empower us to live healthier, happier lives. The good news is that by making positive lifestyle changes, you can help your body cope with stress more effectively.

Key Question To Ask One Self Is*: - "How Much And For How Long Has Stress Been Part Of Daily Life?"*

Raj: Wow, that's serious. So basically, everything I do with my lifestyle – how I eat, how I sleep, how I manage my stress – all of that affects how my body reacts to stress hormones?

Yogi Seshi: Bingo, Raj! You hit the nail on the head. Think of your body like a garden. If you provide it with the right nutrients – healthy food, enough sleep, and regular exercise – it will be strong and resilient. But if you neglect it, feed it junk food, and never let it rest, it becomes vulnerable to weeds and pests – in this case, stress and disease.

Praveen: This workshop is making me rethink my whole lifestyle! I'm excited to learn more about how yoga can help me build a better fire pit, not a raging inferno.

(Laughter fills the room)

Yogi Seshi: (Chuckles) I love that analogy!

Maya: So, what can we do to create a more stress-resistant Body Ville?

Yogi Seshi: That's what the rest of this workshop is all about! We'll be diving deeper into yoga practices, mindfulness techniques, and healthy lifestyle habits that can help you manage stress effectively. The idea isn't to eliminate stress altogether – that's impossible. But it is about learning how to respond to stress in a healthy way, so your Body Ville can weather any storm, a strong foundation for overall well-being. Let's get started with some gentle stretches and breathing exercises to begin calming those internal flames.

David: That sounds awesome! Knowing how stress affects my body actually makes me feel more motivated to manage it. It's not just about feeling better mentally, it's about taking care of my whole system.

Raj: Couldn't agree more. I'm excited to learn how to create a calmer, healthier Body Ville for myself.

Yogi Seshi: (Smiling) Excellent! Let's get started then, shall we? We have a lot to explore!

(The class transitions into the next activity, the students energized and motivated to create a more stress-resistant Body Ville.)

A gentle smile spreads across Yogi Seshi's face as she observes the relaxed expressions of her students, Rishi, Maya, David, Praveen, Alex,, etc. Their shoulders are down, breaths slow and steady, a stark contrast to the animated energy just moments ago.

(She guides the students through a series of gentle yoga postures, focusing on stretches that release tension in the shoulders, neck, and lower back – common stress battlegrounds, later surya namaskar, double breathing, and relaxation.)

Yogi Seshi (softly): "Feel your breath flowing freely, each inhale nourishing your body, each exhale releasing tension."

(They move into a simple seated meditation, focusing on the rise and fall of their abdomens with each breath. The room is filled with a peaceful silence.)

Yogi Seshi (whispering): "Imagine a calming presence within you, a quiet observer of your thoughts and emotions. Let go of any worries that may arise, and simply be present in this moment."

(After a few minutes, Yogi Seshi gently brings the students out of meditation.)

Rishi: (Eyes closed, a contented sigh escaping his lips) Wow, I haven't felt this relaxed in ages. My mind feels... still.

Maya: Me too. It's amazing how a few simple movements and focusing on my breath can make such a difference.

Alex: (Smiling) it's almost like hitting the pause button on the chaos in my head.

Yogi Seshi: (Beaming) Exactly! These practices are powerful tools to calm your nervous system and bring a sense of peace back to Body Ville.

(She pauses, looking at the calendar.)

Yogi Seshi: As much as I'd love to stay here all day in this state of tranquility, we only have one more session left tomorrow.

(The students groan playfully.)

Yogi Seshi (chuckling): Don't worry, it won't be all stress and drama! Tomorrow, we'll delve into the world of lifestyle – how our daily habits can either fuel our inner fire or create a haven of calmness within. We'll explore ancient wisdom and modern science to discover what truly constitutes an ideal lifestyle for stress management and overall well-being.

Maya: Ancient wisdom and science combined? Sounds intriguing!

Rishi: I'm curious to see how the two connect.

Alex: Sign me up!

Yogi Seshi: (Grinning) Excellent! But before you drift off into a blissful sleep tonight, I have one final request.

The students lean forward, intrigued.

Yogi Seshi: Think about what you learned today. Share this knowledge with your family and friends. Talk to them about the stress response, the importance of being aware of your body's signals. See if anything resonates with them. And tomorrow, I'd love to hear some of their insights – their daily struggles with stress, any interesting facts they may discover.

Maya: That's a great idea! My sister has been complaining about constant headaches lately. Maybe understanding the stress connection will help her.

David: My dad always seems on edge. Sharing this knowledge might be a good way to start a conversation.

Alex: I can totally picture my roommate freaking out about "fight or flight"!

(Everyone laughs)

Yogi Seshi: Remember, awareness is the first step to change. By opening up conversations about stress, we can all learn and grow together. Now, get a good night's sleep, and see you all bright-eyed and bushy-tailed... or maybe just relaxed and mindful... tomorrow!

Everyone rolled their mats and kept it in the place for them and enjoying every step forward cheerfully went home.

(The students leave the yoga studio, their bodies lighter, their minds calmer, and a sense of empowerment for their well-being budding within them. They look forward not only to learning more about an ideal lifestyle but also to sharing their newfound knowledge with loved ones, creating ripples of awareness that might change their lives and the lives of those around them.).

End of day 2 workshop

The morning sun cast a warm glow on the city as participants from the stress management workshop emerged, each carrying a newfound perspective. Armed with the knowledge of the body's stress response and practical tools for relaxation, they were eager to integrate these learnings into their lives. But the impact extended beyond their own well-being, as they prepared to share their discoveries with loved ones, fostering a sense of connection and shared support.

From Solo Stress to Shared Serenity

Mark and Sarah Embraces Yoga Together: At the breakfast table, Mark, a graphic designer with a perpetually furrowed brow, nervously glanced at his wife, Sarah. He had always bottled up his stress, but something about the workshop had shifted his perspective.

Mark: Hey Sarah, there's something I wanted to talk about. Remember all that tension I carry in my shoulders? Today at the workshop, we learned how that's actually my body reacting to stress!

Sarah: (Smiling) Oh honey, I know. You could practically build a skyscraper with those shoulders sometimes. What did they say about it?

Mark: Turns out, it's like my body is on high alert, getting ready for a fight-or-flight situation. It's pretty wild! But the best part? They taught us these amazing deep breathing exercises, and guess what? I actually felt calmer after doing them.

Sarah: Really? That's fantastic! I've been wanting you to try yoga for ages. Maybe this is the sign you've been waiting for.

Mark: Maybe you're right. And you know, they were talking about how stress affects sleep too. Remember how I toss and turn all night? Maybe these relaxation techniques could help me get some actual rest for once.

Sarah: They could definitely be worth a try. We could even do them together! Wouldn't that be nice, a little morning yoga ritual just for the two of us?

Mark's brow softened as he smiled at Sarah. The idea of a shared practice, a moment of calm amidst their busy lives, filled him with a sense of peace. He reached for her hand, feeling an unspoken bond strengthened by this newfound understanding.

Teachers Team Up for Student Wellbeing: Across town, at a bustling elementary school, Ms. Sailu, a vibrant teacher, took a deep breath as the bell rang for recess. She met her co-teacher, Mr.Vivek, in the hallway.

Ms. Sailu: Whew! That last class felt like a marathon. It's amazing how even these little ones can get so stressed out.

Mr. Vivek: (Nodding) Tell me about it! The pressure to perform, the constant tests... it's no wonder they get overloaded sometimes.

Ms. Sailu: You know, that stress management workshop yesterday gave me some great ideas. We could try incorporating some simple mindfulness exercises into our classroom routine.

Mr. Vivek: Excellent idea! Maybe some basic stretching or even a short guided meditation could work wonders. Anything to help them identify their stress and learn to manage it.

Ms. Sailu: Exactly! And who knows, maybe it will rub off on us too.

(A sense of camaraderie forms between them as they realize they're not alone in facing stress management challenges within their classroom.)

The Art of Saying No

A Father's Advice on Prioritizing Well-Being: Meanwhile, across the country, Sameer, an accountant, sat at his desk, buried in a mountain of paperwork. He called his father, a retired businessman.

Sameer: Hey Dad, just wanted to check in. How's retirement treating you?

Father: (Chuckling) Peaceful, my son. No more deadlines or endless meetings. Just me, my fishing pole, and a whole lot of serenity.

Sameer: (Sighs) Sounds heavenly. How did you ever manage the stress when you were working full-time?

Father: It wasn't easy, son. But I learned a few things along the way. First, always prioritize sleep. A well-rested mind can handle anything.

Sameer: (Guiltily glances at the clock) Yeah, sleep has been a casualty lately. Work just never seems to stop.

Father: Second, find an outlet for stress. For me, it was fishing. For you, maybe it's painting or playing that guitar you haven't touched in ages.

Sameer: Wow, you remembered that guitar! I miss playing.

Father: Third, and most importantly, learn to say no. You can't do everything, Sameer. Set boundaries and prioritize your well-being.

Sameer: (Nods slowly) you know, Dad, that's actually really good advice. Maybe I need to re-evaluate my workload and learn to say no a little more.

(A sense of gratitude and a renewed respect for his father's wisdom washes over Sameer.)

Sisters Take Flight

A Journey towards Relaxation and Shared Wisdom: In a bustling airport terminal, Anjali, a travel blogger, waited for her flight. She saw her sister, Aarti, approaching, her usually bubbly face etched with worry.

Anjali: Hey Aarti, what's wrong? Travel troubles?

Aarti: (Sighs) Sort of. I just feel so overwhelmed with everything.

Anjali: (Concerned) Sort of? What's going on? You know you can tell me anything.

Aarti: It's just... this constant travel, the pressure to create content, the fear of missing out on something amazing... it all adds up, you know? Sometimes I feel like I'm running on fumes, and I can't remember the last time I truly relaxed.

Anjali: (Places a hand on Aarti's shoulder) Oh honey, I get it. This travel blogger life can be glamorous, but it's definitely not always sunshine and rainbows.

Aarti: Exactly! And then you come along, all Zen and relaxed after this stress management workshop you attended.

Anjali smiles, remembering the insightful discussions and practical tools she learned.

Anjali: Actually, it was pretty amazing! We learned all about how stress affects our bodies and minds, and guess what? There's a whole science behind it!

Atari: (Raises an eyebrow) really? Like, fight-or-flight mode kind of science?

Anjali: (Laughs) Exactly! But even more interesting. We learned simple practices like deep breathing and yoga poses that can actually calm the whole internal chaos down.

Aarti: (Eyes widen) Wait, are you telling me there's a way to silence the inner drama queen and actually relax? Sign me up!

Anjali: Well, not exactly sign you up, but... I did pick up some awesome techniques you could definitely try. Deep breathing exercises, some basic stretches you can do anywhere...

Aarti: (Intrigued) Spill the beans, sis! I'm all ears, and maybe even ready to touch my toes again.

(Anjali spends the next few minutes sharing the key takeaways from the workshop with Aarti, demonstrating some simple breathing techniques and stretches. Aarti listens intently, a spark of hope rekindled in her eyes.)

Aarti: Wow, Anjali, this is amazing! I can't believe I never knew about this stuff before.

Anjali: I know, right? And guess what? The workshop continues tomorrow! They're talking about ideal lifestyles for stress management, a blend of ancient wisdom and modern science.

Aarti: (Eyes gleaming) Ancient wisdom and science? Now that's my kind of travel destination! Maybe they'll even teach us how to find Zen in the middle of a crowded airport terminal.

(They both laugh, a sense of shared understanding and newfound hope for managing their stress bubbling between them.)

Later that night, tucked into her hotel bed, Anjali reviewed the day. She reflected on the insightful conversations with her family, the joy of sharing her newfound knowledge, and the excitement for the next day's session. A sense of peace settled over her as she drifted off to sleep, a calmness that had nothing to do with the luxurious hotel room and everything to do with the empowering tools she now possessed to manage the inevitable stresses of her life.

From Whirlwind to Inner Peace

Rishi's Two-Day Journey of Self-Discovery: As Rishi settled into his meditation posture that evening, a sense of quiet satisfaction washed over him. Two days. Just two days had passed since he'd embarked on this unexpected journey of self-discovery through the yoga workshop. Yet, the shift within him felt profound.

He closed his eyes, and a soft chuckle escaped his lips. "Remember that Rishi from two days ago?" he mused, addressing his inner self. "The one perpetually knotted up with worry, his mind a whirlwind of deadlines and anxieties?"

A gentle silence followed, a silent acknowledgment from within.

"Well," Rishi continued, a smile playing on his lips, "that Rishi seems like a distant memory now. These past two days have been an awakening, a revelation of sorts."

He delved deeper, recounting the workshop's insightful sessions. Yogi Seshi's passionate explanations about the science behind stress, the fascinating connection between his body and mind metaphorically represented as 'Body Ville', the practical tools and techniques they explored - it all played back in his mind like a vivid film.

"It's amazing," he marveled, "how something as simple as a few focused breaths can instantly calm the storm brewing inside. And those yoga poses, though initially awkward, seem to have unlocked a whole new level of flexibility in my body, not to mention a surprising sense of ease."

He paused, reflecting on the subtle changes he'd incorporated into his workday. "Taking a short walk during my lunch break, away from the screen and the incessant emails, has done wonders for clearing my head," he admitted. "And those few minutes of deep breathing at my desk, eyes closed, actually helped me tackle that complex report with a newfound focus."

A sense of accomplishment filled him. These simple adjustments, woven into the fabric of his day, had a profound impact.

"It's not a magic bullet, of course," he conceded, "but it's a start. A conscious effort to break free from the autopilot mode and acknowledge the signals my body is sending."

As if on cue, a gentle breeze rustled through the open window, carrying with it a sense of serenity. Rishi felt a deep sense of gratitude for this unexpected turn of events.

Suddenly, a yogi's powerful quote, gleaned from Yogi Seshi's closing remarks, echoed within him:

"Inner peace and outer dynamism can go hand in hand." The words resonated deeply. Yes, the power to manage stress, to cultivate inner peace, resided within him all along. The workshop had simply served as a catalyst, a reminder of his own inherent strength and resilience.

Rishi smiled, a newfound awareness blooming within him. He was no longer just Rishi, the stressed-out Country head. He was, the observer, the conscious being, capable of harnessing the power within to create a life of greater balance and harmony. And that, he realized, was a journey worth taking, one mindful breath, and one mindful step at a time.

CHAPTER 4

Sacred and Scientific: The Lifestyle Connection

Day 3 of Workshop

Embracing the Present Moment: As Rishi approached the familiar space for the final day of the workshop, a sense of calm anticipation washed over him. He paused for a moment, taking in the serene scene before him.

A glistening pond shimmered to his left, its surface a mirror reflecting the vibrant hues of the rising sun. Delicate lotus flowers, some in full bloom, others still tightly furled in potential, graced the water's edge. Their gentle sway in the soft breeze mirrored the newfound peace blossoming within Rishi.

A symphony of chirps and twitters filled the air as a kaleidoscope of birds flitted between the branches of a nearby tree. Some dipped their beaks into the nectar of brightly colored flowers, while others, with a flurry of activity, built their nests or diligently fed their young. The sight awakened a sense of wonder within Rishi, a reminder of the interconnectedness of all living things.

With each step on the soft grass, a gentle sensation tickled his bare feet. The earthy aroma of damp mud mingled with the sweet fragrance of blooming flowers, creating a unique and grounding perfume. It was a sensory experience that brought him fully into the present moment.

A gentle breeze rustled through the leaves, carrying with it a whisper of serenity. Rishi closed his eyes for a moment, allowing the sound to wash over him, a calming counterpoint to the usual cacophony of his daily life.

In that quiet space, surrounded by the beauty of nature, Rishi felt a profound sense of peace. His body, relaxed and grounded, seemed to resonate with the tranquil environment. This wasn't just awareness of his surroundings; it was a deep connection, a feeling of belonging to a greater whole. He was no longer just present; he was truly present, and present within.

With a renewed sense of purpose and a heart filled with gratitude, Rishi entered the workshop space, ready to embrace the final lessons on his journey towards a more stress-managed life. The day promised to be a culmination of the past two days, a final piece to the puzzle that would empower him to navigate the inevitable challenges life threw his way with newfound resilience and inner peace. As Rishi stepped into the workshop space, a calming aroma of lavender and lemongrass wafted through the air. Gone were the usual chairs; instead, colorful yoga mats were spread out, inviting a more relaxed and introspective atmosphere. Soft, melodic chanting music played in the background, further setting the tone for the final day.

Many participants were already gathered, chatting in hushed tones, a sense of anticipation hanging in the air. Yogi Seshi, the workshop facilitator, stood at the front of the room, a warm smile gracing her face. She wore a simple white kurta pajama, her posture radiating serenity.

Yogi Seshi: (Gently ringing a small bell) Good morning everyone, and welcome to the final day of our rejuvenation workshop! I hope you all enjoyed the past two days of learning and exploration. Today, we delve deeper into the heart of the matter – the philosophy of stress, and how it manifests in our lives. We'll explore the science behind healthy lifestyles and how ancient yogic practices can become powerful tools to combat chronic stress.

(She pauses, looking around the room, her gaze meeting Rishi's.)

Yogi Seshi: (Smiling warmly) Rishi, you seem particularly centered this morning. Would you like to share how your practice has been so far?

A gentle blush crept up Rishi's neck, but he surprised himself by nodding.

Rishi: (Softly) thank you, Yogi Seshi. It's been an eye-opening experience. Learning about the internal responses to stress has helped me understand what's been happening within me. And the breathing exercises and yoga poses – well, they've been surprisingly calming.

Yogi Seshi: (Beaming) that's wonderful to hear, Rishi! Remember, the journey towards a stress-free life is a continuous process. But by incorporating simple practices like breathing exercises and mindful movement into your daily routine, you can make significant strides.

(She turns back to the group, her voice filled with enthusiasm.)

Yogi Seshi: Now, to truly understand stress, we need to go beyond just the physical symptoms. Let's start our day with a short meditation exercise. Close your eyes, find a comfortable seated position, and focus on your breath. Feel the rise and fall of your chest with each inhale and exhale. As thoughts arise, acknowledge them gently and let them go, like clouds passing across a vast blue sky. Let's spend a few minutes simply being present in this moment.

(The room falls silent as everyone settles into their meditation. A gentle smile plays on Yogi Seshi's lips as she observes the focused faces. A few minutes pass, punctuated only by the soft sound of breath.)

Yogi Seshi: (Softly) slowly bring your awareness back to the room. Notice how your body feels – relaxed, grounded, centered. This is the state we strive to cultivate throughout our day, even amidst life's inevitable challenges.

(The workshop continues, weaving together insightful discussions on the philosophy and science of stress with practical yogic techniques. Rishi, along with the other participants, actively engages, asking questions and sharing experiences. The day feels less like a class and more like a collaborative exploration, a journey towards creating a toolbox for a healthier, more balanced way of life.)

Yogi Seshi stands at the front of the workshop space, a warm smile gracing her face. The participants, having spent the past two days exploring stress management techniques, are eager to learn more.

Yogi Seshi: Today, before we delve deeper into the topic: a quick recap on lifestyle diseases. These chronic conditions, like hypertension, diabetes, and heart disease, are on the rise globally.

(A murmur of curiosity ripples through the room.)

Yogi Seshi: Modern medicine may not always find an infectious agent or a specific physical dysfunction in these cases. The culprit often lies in a more subtle realm – our lifestyle choices.

(She turns towards Maya, a participant.)

Yogi Seshi: Maya, as we discussed yesterday, our world seems fixated on speed, materialism, and constant pressure. These external factors can easily influence us, leading to stress, anxiety, and unhealthy coping mechanisms.

Maya: Absolutely! The constant deadlines, the pressure to succeed, it can all feel overwhelming sometimes.

Yogi Seshi: Exactly, and it's not just external pressures. Our natural instinct is for comfort and pleasure, but sometimes we seek it in unhealthy ways - poor diet, lack of exercise, unethical means. These choices, ironically, lead to more stress and unhappiness in the long run.

David: (Another participant) Yes, I now understand that our lifestyle choices are making us physically sick

Yogi Seshi: Yes! David, that's exactly what research suggests. Studies show a strong correlation between several lifestyle factors and the prevalence of chronic diseases. Think about it – of the world population nearly31% of adults and 80% of adolescents do not meet the recommended levels of physical activity. These factors like lack of physical activity and healthy diet coupled with long working hours and societal pressures, create a perfect storm for our health.

But the good news is, we have the power to change course! By making conscious choices about our lifestyle, we can create a foundation of resilience that protects us from the negative effects of stress.

(Yogi Seshi pauses for a moment, allowing the information to sink in. She then transitions smoothly into presenting the scientific research articles, delving into the fascinating interplay between stress, lifestyle, and chronic disease.)

Let's now explore how conscious lifestyle choices can empower us to manage stress and cultivate vibrant health.

(She pauses, her eyes twinkling.)

Yogi Seshi: Did you know that a groundbreaking study by Dr. Dean Ornish revealed a remarkable truth about the power of lifestyle changes?

(A murmur of curiosity ripples through the room. She points to the graph.)

Yogi Seshi: This fascinating study, conducted by Dr. Dean Ornish, focused on individuals with significant heart disease. The research demonstrated a powerful truth: comprehensive lifestyle changes can actually reverse artery blockages! (A murmur of surprise ripples through the audience.)

Yogi Seshi: Yes, you heard that right! The study involved a group of patients who adopted a low-fat vegetarian diet, quit smoking, incorporated stress management techniques, and engaged in moderate exercise. The results, after just one year, were interesting. These individuals experienced a reversal of coronary atherosclerosis, a condition due to plaque buildup in the arteries, without resorting to medications!

David: (A participant, eyes wide with interest) Wow! That's incredible. Who would have thought a change in lifestyle could have such a dramatic impact?

Yogi Seshi: It's a testament to the power we hold within ourselves, David. Our bodies possess an incredible capacity for healing and resilience. By making conscious choices about what we eat, how we move our bodies, and how we manage stress, we can significantly improve our health and well-being.

Understanding Yoga: The Science behind Its Benefits

(Yogi Seshi stands before the workshop participants, a bright light illuminating the room. A diagram depicting the human brain and nervous system adorns the screen behind her.)

Yogi Seshi: Now, let's delve into the scientific evidence behind yoga's remarkable impact on stress reduction. We've all experienced the calming effects of yoga firsthand, but what exactly happens within us that fosters this sense of peace?

(She gestures to the brain diagram.)

Yogi Seshi: This topic has piqued the interest of scientists around the world. Research shows that yoga is increasingly being used in clinical settings to address a variety of mental and physical health concerns, particularly those related to stress. And the results are undeniably promising!

(A sense of anticipation fills the room.)

Yogi Seshi: However, the exact mechanisms through which yoga reduces stress have remained somewhat of a mystery. Fortunately, recent research is shedding light on this fascinating interplay between yoga and our well-being. A comprehensive study conducted by a team of researchers examined the ways in which yoga impacts stress on a deeper level.

(She pauses, emphasizing the key points.)

Yogi Seshi: Through a rigorous review of existing research, they identified seven key mechanisms:

- Psychological Mechanisms: These involve changes in our emotional state and self-perception. Yoga practices cultivate positive affect, fostering optimism and a more positive outlook. Additionally, they promote self-compassion, encouraging us to treat ourselves with kindness and understanding.

These shifts in perspective significantly reduce stress and anxiety.

- Biological Mechanisms: The study also revealed fascinating biological factors at play. Yoga practices seem to inhibit the activity of the posterior hypothalamus, a region in the brain responsible for the stress response. This translates to a decrease in the production of stress hormones like cortisol. Furthermore, yoga can potentially influence the levels of interleukin-6 and C-reactive protein, inflammatory markers linked to stress.

(David, a participant, raises his hand, his eyes filled with curiosity.)

David: So, yoga isn't just about feeling good in the moment – it actually changes our bodies' response to stress?

Yogi Seshi: Exactly, David! Yoga's holistic approach addresses both psychological and biological aspects of stress, creating a powerful synergy that benefits our health and well-being in profound ways.

(Maya, another participant, leans forward, eager to learn more.)

Maya: This research adds a whole new layer of understanding to the benefits of yoga! It's exciting to see science catching up with what we've been experiencing all along.

Yogi Seshi: Absolutely, Maya! This growing body of research validates the effectiveness of yoga as a powerful stress management tool. By understanding these mechanisms, we can deepen our appreciation for yoga and confidently integrate these practices into our daily lives for lasting well-being.

(The workshop continues with Yogi Seshi exploring the limitations of the current research and the need for further exploration of yoga's impact. She emphasizes the importance of personal experience.)

Taking Charge

Putting Knowledge into Action

Yogi Seshi: As we reach the final stretch of our journey together, I want to acknowledge the incredible progress you've all made. Over the past two days, we've delved deep into the science of stress, explored ancient yogic wisdom, and most importantly, experienced the transformative power of these practices firsthand.

(She pauses, allowing a sense of accomplishment to settle over the room.)

Yogi Seshi: We've discussed the critical role of ideal lifestyle choices, the cornerstone of managing stress and cultivating well-being. We explored the scientific evidence behind this concept, and I know these insights resonated deeply with all of you.

(She holds up a stack of neatly folded papers.)

Yogi Seshi: To reinforce these powerful messages, I've prepared a detailed handout that further explains the principles of an ideal yogic lifestyle. I urge you to read it thoroughly tonight, and at most by the weekend. It's filled with practical tips and information that will serve as a valuable resource on your journey.

(A sense of anticipation fills the room.)

Yogi Seshi: Now, here's where the true magic happens! I've created an exclusive online community group specifically for all of you, our amazing workshop participants. This will be a safe space to share your experiences, ask questions, and offer support to one another. Remember, we're all in this together!

(She beams at the group.)

Yogi Seshi: This is more than just a workshop; it's the start of a supportive community. Imagine the power of learning from each other, celebrating successes, and facing challenges together. This group will be your platform to do just that.

(She leans forward, her voice filled with conviction.)

Yogi Seshi: "*The journey of a thousand miles begins with a single step,*" says Lao Tzu. Let's take that first step together. Let's commit to integrating these principles into our daily lives, one mindful breath, and one conscious choice at a time.

As Mahatma Gandhi beautifully said, "*Be the change that you wish to see in the world.*" Take ownership of your well-being. Apply the knowledge you've gained to create a life rooted in resilience and inner peace. Use the community group as a catalyst for shared growth and support.

(The participants nod enthusiastically, their faces alight with excitement and newfound purpose.)

Yogi Seshi: Now, with all this inspiration buzzing in our hearts, let's prepare for the final activities of the day! We'll have one last chance to practice some powerful yoga techniques, solidify your understanding through interactive exercises, and most importantly, create a personalized action plan to carry this knowledge into your daily lives. Remember, your journey towards a stress-free and fulfilling life starts now!

Activity Hour

Group Activity: Identifying Stressors and Crafting Solutions (15-20 minutes)

Yogi Seshi: Alright everyone, in this activity we'll be delving deeper into your personal stress landscape. Let's work in small groups to brainstorm common stressors you encounter in your daily lives and explore healthy coping mechanisms to address them.

(She looks around the room, counting participants.)

Yogi Seshi: We have a total of 50 participants today. To ensure everyone has a chance to contribute, let's create ten groups of five people each. Feel free to mingle and find four others to form your groups.

(She allows a few moments for participants to form their groups.)

Yogi Seshi: Great! Once you've settled into your groups, here's what we'll be doing:

a) Brainstorm Stressors (5 minutes): Take the first five minutes to discuss and list as many common stressors you face in your daily lives. Think about work, family, finances, social situations, health, or anything else that creates tension or anxiety. The goal is to create a comprehensive list that reflects the different challenges each of you experience. Later, Coping strategies.

b) Craft Coping Strategies (10 minutes): Now, let's shift our focus to solutions. For each stressor you listed, brainstorm at least two healthy coping mechanisms. Think about what techniques or strategies you've already tried that worked well, or consider practices learned throughout the workshop, such as yoga poses, breathing exercises, mindfulness techniques, communication skills, or time management strategies. Be creative and explore different approaches. Finally; Share.

c) Share and Discuss (5 minutes): Once you have a list of stressors with corresponding coping mechanisms, take turns sharing your list with the larger group. This allows everyone to learn from each other's insights and discover new ways to manage stress.

Yogi Seshi: Remember, there are no right or wrong answers here. The key is to identify what works for you and explore various options. I'll be setting a timer for fifteen minutes for the group activity, followed by five minutes for everyone to share their learnings. So, let's dive in!

(Yogi Seshi sets a timer and observes the participants as they engage in lively discussions within their groups. She circulates the room, offering guidance and encouragement if needed. After the allotted time, she signals for everyone's attention.)

Yogi Seshi: Alright everyone, time's up! Let's hear some insights from your groups. Who would like to volunteer to share their list of stressors and coping mechanisms?

Learning Together, Growing Stronger

Yogi Seshi: David, would you mind sharing a key takeaway from your group?

David: Absolutely! One stressor that resonated with everyone was the feeling of being overwhelmed at work. We all agreed that constant deadlines and long hours were major culprits. However, one person in our group suggested a time management technique called the "Eisenhower Matrix." It helps categorize tasks based on urgency and importance, allowing for better prioritization and reducing the feeling of being overbooked. We all agreed to try it out this week!

Yogi Seshi: Excellent! The Eisenhower Matrix can be a powerful tool for managing workload. Maya, what did your group discover?

Maya: Our group discussed the stress of juggling family responsibilities alongside personal needs. We realized the importance of setting boundaries and clear communication. One person shared how practicing mindful breathing exercises before talking to her children helped her communicate more calmly and effectively. We also discussed the importance of scheduling self-care time, even if it's just 15 minutes a day for reading or meditation.

Yogi Seshi: Those are wonderful solutions, Maya. Mindfulness practices and self-care are crucial for stress management. Sarah, what did your group find most helpful?

Sarah: We talked a lot about social media and the pressure to maintain a perfect online persona. Several of us found it contributed to feelings of inadequacy. One person suggested a digital detox – taking a break from social media for a few days. Another person mentioned a practice of gratitude journaling, focusing on the positive aspects of their lives. We all agreed to be more mindful of our social media consumption and focus on fostering real-life connections.

Yogi Seshi: Fantastic points, Sarah! Social media detox and gratitude journaling are excellent strategies for reducing comparison and boosting self-esteem. These are all great examples of how we can personalize the tools and techniques learned in this workshop to address our individual stressors. Remember, the key is to experiment and find what works best for you.

Does anyone else have an experience they'd like to share?

Jessica (participant, raising her hand): Yes, if that's okay. I realized during our group discussion that a lot of my stress stems from negative self-talk. I constantly criticize myself for not being good enough at work, and I compare myself to others on social media, which just makes me feel worse. To be honest, I haven't even acknowledged how much chronic stress I'm under until this workshop. For years, I've been feeling overwhelmed and stressed, but I never really admitted it to myself. I just kept pushing through, telling myself I should be able to handle everything. For example, if I make a mistake at work, I'll beat myself up and call myself names. It creates this cycle of stress and negativity that's hard to break free from. On top of that, I've been feeling constantly on edge lately – like I can't relax, even when I have free time. It's been affecting my sleep, my relationships, and my overall well-being. Today's workshop helped me realize that I'm not alone, and more importantly, that there are tools I can use to manage my stress and silence that negative voice in my head.

Yogi Seshi: Jessica, thank you for sharing so openly. It's truly inspiring to see this level of self-awareness. It's important to recognize negative self-talk and its impact on our stress levels. Many of us struggle with that inner critic.

David: (another participant) I completely understand. I do the same thing to myself sometimes.

Yogi Seshi: Yes, David, it's common. But the good news is that there are ways to address it. Yoga and mindfulness practices can help you cultivate self-compassion and challenge those negative thoughts. Also, remember the importance of surrounding yourself with supportive people who uplift you, rather than comparing yourself to unrealistic portrayals on social media.

Jessica: That's really helpful, Yogi Seshi. I think focusing on self-compassion and staying away from social media for a while could be good first steps for me.

Yogi Seshi: Absolutely, Jessica. And remember, you're not alone in this. We're all here to support each other on this journey.

(The workshop continues with Yogi Seshi offering additional guidance on managing negative self-talk and chronic stress through yoga practices, mindfulness techniques, and building a supportive network. The workshop is nearing its conclusion. Participants have shared their insights from the group activity, and Yogi Seshi invites one last volunteer.)

Unveiling the Fog: Understanding Stress and Memory

Yogi Seshi: Is there anyone else who'd like to share a key takeaway from their group discussion?

Mark: (Participant, raises his hand thoughtfully) Yes, actually. Our group had a fascinating conversation with Ms. Sailu who explained the science behind our experiences with stress and memory and research study related to it. It really resonated with me. We were talking about how stress can affect memory and focus, and it suddenly made a lot of sense. She explained that this might be due to the impact of stress on two key areas of our brain – the prefrontal cortex and the hippocampus.

Yogi Seshi: Please, elaborate, Mark. Your experience might resonate with others.

Mark: Well, for the past few months, I've been feeling like I'm in a fog. It's hard to concentrate at work, and I can't seem to remember even simple things. I even struggled to recall some of the concepts we learned earlier in the workshop. I just felt scattered and overwhelmed.

(Mark gestures towards a flipchart where Yogi Seshi has sketched a simple diagram of the brain.)

Mark: The prefrontal cortex, also called the frontal lobe, is kind of like the CEO of our brain. It helps us set goals, organize our thoughts, plan, and prioritize tasks. It's also crucial for working memory, which is like our mental notepad, holding information for short-term use. Ms. Sailu mentioned, "The prefrontal cortex is the difference between 'Why did I do that? And I planned to do that."

(A ripple of understanding flows through the room.)

Mark: Now, imagine this CEO under pressure. Research suggests that during chronic stress, the prefrontal cortex gets overloaded, like a computer shutting down. This can explain why we struggle to focus, make decisions, and even remember the valuable information we learn in workshops like this!

Yogi Seshi: That's a fantastic point, Mark. Stress hormones like cortisol can literally shrink the prefrontal cortex, impacting its functionality.

Mark: Exactly! The other area we discussed was the hippocampus, which is the memory powerhouse of the brain. It's like our brain's filing cabinet, storing and retrieving information. Just like the prefrontal cortex, the hippocampus is also vulnerable to stress. High stress levels can damage its delicate connections, making it harder for us to form new memories or recall existing ones.

Yogi Seshi: This scientific explanation sheds light on why we might feel like our brains are foggy during stressful periods. But did your group discuss any solutions, Mark?

Mark: Absolutely! The good news is that the brain is remarkably plastic. With the right strategies, we can strengthen these areas and improve our cognitive function. And guess what the key is? Being active!

(Mark emphasizes the last point with a smile.)

Mark: Exercise, particularly aerobic exercise, has been shown to increase blood flow to the brain, nourishing these crucial areas. It also promotes the growth of new brain cells and strengthens existing connections. So, while stress can put our brain on hold, staying active is like hitting the reset button!

(Yogi Seshi smiles warmly at Mark, his insightful contribution resonating with the group.)

Yogi Seshi: That's a powerful message, Mark. "There is a way out – It is to be 'Active'" – a fantastic way to summarize the connection between stress, memory, and the power of an active lifestyle. Thank you for sharing this insightful perspective. Here, at this juncture would like to emphasize The Power of Pranayama

Yogi Seshi: once again, thank you Mark, for that insightful explanation! Understanding how stress impacts the brain is a powerful step towards managing it. And as we've explored throughout this workshop, yoga offers a variety of tools to combat stress and enhance our cognitive function. One particularly powerful technique is pranayama, yogic breathing practices.

(Yogi Seshi walks towards a table where a yoga mat and a small model of the brain are placed.)

Yogi Seshi: As our ancient texts say, "All the yogic practices purify prana," the vital life force that flows through us. Pranayama is like the crown jewel of these practices, specifically targeting the control and regulation of breath. By consciously extending and slowing down our inhalations and exhalations (to our capacity, but never to the point of forcing), we set off a cascade of beneficial effects.

(She picks up the model of the brain and points to a specific area.)

Yogi Seshi: Typically, our breath is controlled by the medulla oblongata, a part of the brainstem responsible for basic functions. However, through conscious pranayama, we activate the prefrontal cortex, the CEO of our brain as Mark mentioned earlier. This shift empowers us to respond rather than react to stressful situations.

(Yogi Seshi places the model back on the table. She shares 3 powerful pranayama practices.)

Yogi Seshi: Remember how we discussed the left and right hemispheres of the brain? Pranayama practices like alternate nostril breathing (Anulom Vilom) help balance the activity of these hemispheres, which are connected to our sympathetic and parasympathetic nervous systems. The sympathetic nervous system is responsible for the fight-or-flight response, while the parasympathetic nervous system promotes relaxation and well-being. By balancing these opposing forces, pranayama creates a state of inner calm and clarity, even amidst stressful circumstances.

Now, let's explore yet another powerful yogic breathing technique called "double breathing," Imagine inhaling twice one short and the second long breath, filling your lower and the upper lungs. Then, like a wave receding from the shore, exhale slowly and completely out through the mouth. This simple practice, my friends, is a gateway to inner peace. By eliminating excess carbon dioxide and calming your heart rate, double breathing activates the relaxation response within minutes. In just a few breaths, you can feel tension melt away, leaving you centered, focused, and ready to tackle whatever life throws your way. So next time stress creeps in, take a moment, and try double breathing. You might be surprised by its transformative power.

Yogi Seshi: (Smiling warmly) now, let's delve into the very essence of pranayama, the foundation upon which all other breathing techniques build: deep breathing. Simple, yet profoundly powerful.

(Yogi Seshi demonstrates the breath with slow, exaggerated movements)

Yogi Seshi: Inhale deeply, feeling your abdomen expand as if filling a balloon. Feel the life force, the prana, coursing through your body. Now, exhale slowly, completely, releasing any tension like a sigh. Relax, reeeelaaaaxxxx. (She emphasizes the "relax" with a gentle lengthening of the word)

Yogi Seshi: Did you know, my friends, that our breath is a mirror to our emotions? When stressed, it becomes shallow and rapid. But with conscious deep breathing, we can shift gears, calming the mind and body.

But how do we integrate this practice into our daily lives? That's where habit stacking comes in. Imagine this: every time you reach for a glass of water, take a deep, mindful breath beforehand. Answering a phone call? Another deep breath to center yourself. Opening a door? Inhale deeply, exhale, relax, and step into a calmer space.

Yogi Seshi: (She walks around the room, placing colorful sticky notes," Take a deep breath, exhale and relax" on visible surfaces) Let these little reminders be your guides. Stick them in your bathroom, your workspace, even the refrigerator! Every time you see the sticky note, take that action. Practice this deep breathing throughout your day, and gradually, it will become second nature.

(Her gaze meets each participant) Please, don't underestimate the power of this simple practice. It can be the anchor in your storm, the pause that refreshes, the key to unlocking a calmer, more balanced you. In just a few weeks, you'll be amazed at the difference it makes. You become calm and composed, more productive. You'll thank yourselves for integrating this practice into your lives.

(Yogi Seshi smiles, her eyes twinkling with encouragement.)

Yogi Seshi: So, while exercise is a fantastic way to boost brain function, pranayama offers a targeted approach to activating the prefrontal cortex and promoting nervous system balance. This is why it's such a powerful tool for stress management and overall well-being.

(Yogi Seshi continues by explaining different pranayama techniques and their benefits, further empowering participants to integrate these practices into their daily lives.)

Closing Ceremony: Embracing a Yogic Journey

(Yogi Seshi stands before the participants, a warm smile radiating from her face.)

Yogi Seshi: We have come to the final leg of our incredible journey together! These three days have been filled with exploration, learning, and most importantly, self-discovery. We delved into the fascinating world of yoga, uncovering its profound impact on stress management and overall well-being.

(She pauses, looking around the room at the faces of the participants.)

Yogi Seshi: Remember, stress isn't just about external pressures. It's also about the way we choose to respond to them. Through yoga, we've explored a yogic perspective – a holistic approach that considers the mind, body, and spirit. We learned how unhealthy lifestyle choices can exacerbate stress, while mindful practices like yoga postures, pranayama (breath work), and meditation can nurture a state of balance, resilience, and inner peace.

(She holds up a printed handout.)

Yogi Seshi: As mentioned earlier, this resource booklet summarizes the key concepts we've covered. It includes information on yogic practices, dietary recommendations, and stress management techniques. I encourage you to visit the link provided in this handout. It delves deeper into the yogic philosophy of a healthy and vibrant life, offering additional practices and resources to continue your journey beyond this workshop. Use this booklet and the resources shared in our online community group to integrate these practices into your daily life towards a transformative journey.

(She gestures towards a laptop displaying the online community group page.)

Yogi Seshi: Remember, the community group is here for you. Share your experiences, ask questions, and offer support to your fellow yogis. Together, we can continue to learn and grow on this path of well-being.

(A sense of camaraderie fills the room.)

Yogi Seshi: Now, let's conclude our time together with a final practice – a guided Yoga Nidra. This deep relaxation technique will allow you to integrate the learnings of this workshop on a deeper level. Find a comfortable position, close your eyes, and prepare to embark on a journey within.

(Yogi Seshi guides the participants through a beautifully crafted Yoga Nidra session, weaving soothing imagery and gentle instructions that allow them to release tension, cultivate peace, and connect with their inner resources.)

(As the practice concludes, Yogi Seshi gently brings the participants back to the present moment.)

Yogi Seshi: May you carry the peace and wisdom of this workshop into your daily life. Remember, stress is inevitable, but how you respond to it is your choice. Choose wisely, choose yoga! And on that playful note, remember

"Three days of deep breaths, mindful movements, and 'Oms' to last a lifetime! Let's leave our stress here and take home the peace." - Yogi Seshi"

(A wave of laughter ripples through the room.)

Yogi Seshi: With that lighthearted sentiment, I bid you farewell and wish you all a life filled with health, happiness, and vibrant well-being. Go forth and shine!

(The workshop officially concludes, leaving a lasting impression on the participants. They depart feeling empowered to manage stress, cultivate inner peace, and lead a more joyful and fulfilling life.)

The day's work had been a whirlwind, emails buzzing, deadlines looming. Yet, a subtle shift had taken place within Rishi. As he stepped through his apartment door, the weight he usually carried felt lighter. A sense of calm, a new perspective, lingered from the workshop.

He shed his work clothes, the familiar tightness in his shoulders easing with each layer removed. Suddenly, his eyes fell on the booklet nestled on his bedside table – the one gifted by the yogi Seshi at the end of the session. A smile, genuine and warm, graced his lips. He remembered her words, "The key lies in integrating these practices into your daily lives."

With a quiet anticipation, Rishi settled into bed and opened the booklet. The words danced before his eyes, not as foreign concepts anymore, but as practical tools waiting to be explored. He delved into the yogic philosophy, the in-depth explanations resonating with the experiences from the workshop. He learned about the importance of cultivating inner balance, the power of conscious breath, and the transformative potential of yoga practices.

As he read, a sense of peace washed over him. His eyelids began to grow heavy, the words blurring on the page. The knowledge he was absorbing wasn't just intellectual; it seeped into his very being. A contented sigh escaped his lips as sleep gently claimed him. His inner self, a silent observer, watched with a sense of joy and accomplishment. The lines of worry that had etched his face were replaced by a profound serenity. This wasn't just a peaceful sleep; it was the beginning of a transformation.

Rishi's journey with yoga had just begun, and the path ahead held immense promise. His inner self, filled with a newfound optimism, knew that with each step, with each practice, Rishi would move closer to a life of well-being, a life filled with the peace he was experiencing in this very moment.

CHAPTER 5

Building a Balanced Life

Rishi logs in, Scrolling through the community online group. He reads:

"A genuine smile distributes the cosmic current, Prana, to every body cell. The happy man is less subject to disease, for happiness actually attracts into the body a greater supply of the Universal life energy." – Sri Paramahansa Yogananda

He sees his fellow participants from the workshop actively sharing their takeaways from the booklet. Aanya (One friend) writes about a newfound appreciation for mindfulness and how she is incorporating meditation into their daily routine.

Another (Mike) shares a passage that resonated with him about the power of yogic sleep and positive affirmations, "I am learning to listen to my body and honor its needs."

Seeing their enthusiasm, Rishi feels a surge of motivation. He realizes he drifted off while reading earlier, perhaps due to the relaxed weekend atmosphere compared to his usual workaholic self. Feeling determined, he types a message:

"Wow, seeing everyone's posts is so inspiring! I started reading the booklet last night but ended up falling asleep. (Weekend relaxation, you know?) I'm going to give it another go now, uninterrupted this time. Really looking forward to diving deeper!" Presses send. He puts his phone away, settles back comfortably, and immerses himself back into the yogic wisdom, eager to learn and grow.

Yogi Seshi Priya

Founder of Oneness Academy

Yogi Seshi, a seasoned yoga therapist, brings a wealth of knowledge and experience to her role as the founder of Oneness Academy. With a deep-rooted passion for holistic well-being, she has dedicated her life to exploring the transformative power of yoga.

Yogi Seshi is a seasoned practitioner with a deep understanding of the mind-body connection. She guides students on transformative journeys through yoga, creating a supportive space for growth.

Oneness Academy, under her visionary leadership, offers a sanctuary for seekers. Our comprehensive yoga programs, workshops, and retreats cater to all levels, fostering inner peace, balance, and harmony.

"Embark on a transformative journey to a healthier, more balanced you. This comprehensive guide explores the nature of stress, its impact on your well-being, and the power of yoga to restore harmony. Delve into the science behind stress, understand its various forms, and discover practical yogic techniques to cultivate inner peace and resilience."

What you'll learn:
- ❖ Demystifying Stress
- ❖ Navigating Stress Types: Acute, Chronic, and More
- ❖ Cracking the Stress Code: Triggers Are the Key
- ❖ From Stress to Harmony
- ❖ Unveiling the Power of Yoga: Tools and Techniques for Stress Relief

Techniques:

- ❖ Pancha Kosha Healing
- ❖ Ashtanga Yoga
- ❖ Quick De-Stress daily routine
- ❖ Kriya Yoga
- ❖ Pratipaksha Bhavanam
- ❖ Saakshi bhava
- ❖ Abhyasa
- ❖ Yogic Lifestyle

STRESS

Is my stress response "helpful" or "harmful"?

Feeling stressed? You're not alone! Stress is a natural reaction to challenging situations, but too much of it can take a toll on your health and well-being.

This guide will break down the different types of stress, what causes it, and how yoga can help you manage it effectively.

WHAT IS STRESS? Ever feel like you're stuck in a rocking chair, busy but not getting anywhere? That's a great way to think about stress. It's a feeling of being out of sync with your present situation. As Eckhart Tolle explains: "Stress is caused by being 'here' but wanting to be 'there."

Stress can be caused by both external factors, like work deadlines or financial problems, and internal factors, like negative self-talk.

Navigating Different Types of Stress: How does stress affect my thoughts and emotions? Do my thoughts and emotions impact my physical health? Let's understand.

Stress comes in many forms, each with its own impact. Each type affects us differently, and the key to managing stress lies in understanding its different forms.

Distress: This is the overwhelming feeling that hits when demands become too much. It can lead to anxiety, sadness, and exhaustion.

Acute Stress: The Immediate Jolt

Imagine yourself bungee jumping. That initial surge of adrenaline and alertness as you take the leap — that's acute stress. It's a short-term response to a sudden challenge, like a presentation at work or an unexpected car horn. Our bodies react by releasing hormones like cortisol, sharpening our senses and giving us a burst of energy to deal with the situation. Think of it like a rubber band – it stretches (increases stress) to meet the immediate demand, but then snaps back to its normal state (relaxation) once the challenge is over. This is the positive kind of stress (Eustress) that motivates you to do your best.

Chronic Stress: The Rubber Band Snaps (Analogy: The Overstretched Rubber Band)
Now, imagine holding that same rubber band taut for hours on end. It gets tiring, right? That's chronic stress. It's the prolonged exposure to stressors, like a demanding job, financial woes, or a troubled relationship. Unlike acute stress, chronic stress doesn't have a clear endpoint. The constant tension can lead to physical and emotional problems like headaches, anxiety, and depression. Just like an overstretched rubber band loses its elasticity, chronic stress can leave us feeling depleted and vulnerable.

Episodic acute stress (daily hassles), traumatic stress (deeply disturbing events), and chronic stressors (pollution, crowding) can all drain our energy. Our thoughts, worries, and physical challenges can also contribute to stress. Understanding these types is key to managing stress and promoting well-being.

By understanding these different types of stress and their impact, we can develop a toolbox of strategies to manage them effectively. Yoga, with its emphasis on awareness, cleansing processes, pranayama techniques, movement, and mindfulness, offers a powerful approach to reducing stress, bringing about balance and cultivating inner peace.

Cracking the Stress Code

Triggers and the Body's Response: Solving the Stress puzzle, the first piece is to find a solution by identifying your triggers. These are the events, situations, or even people that set off your stress response. They can be anything from work deadlines to financial worries, relationship issues, or health concerns.

Why identify your triggers? Simple – once you know what pushes your buttons, by understanding the link between triggers, the body's physiological response, and the resulting symptoms, you gain a powerful tool: the ability to manage stress before it manages you.

The Body's Stress Response: Orchestrating Action

The human body responds to stress in a complex, coordinated way. When a threat is perceived, the hypothalamus, a region in the brain, acts as the conductor. It triggers a cascade of hormonal signals. First, the hypothalamus releases Corticotropin-releasing hormone (CRH). This hormone acts as a messenger, traveling to the pituitary gland. The pituitary gland, in turn, releases Adrenocorticotropic hormone (ACTH).

Finally, ACTH reaches the adrenal glands, located atop the kidneys. These glands respond by releasing a surge of stress hormones, primarily cortisol and adrenaline.

The Symphony of Stress Hormones:

- Adrenaline: This hormone increases heart rate and blood pressure, ensuring a rapid flow of oxygen and nutrients to vital muscles.

- Cortisol: Often referred to as the "stress hormone," cortisol plays a multifaceted role. It increases blood sugar levels for immediate energy, enhances the brain's use of glucose, and suppresses non-essential functions like digestion and growth.

The Cost of Chronic Stress

While this "fight-or-flight" response is essential for short-term survival, chronic stress can have detrimental effects on the body when the orchestra continues to play for too long. Here are some key consequences:

- Disrupted Hormone Regulation: Constant cortisol release can throw other hormone systems out of balance.
- Physical Strain: Elevated heart rate and muscle tension can lead to fatigue and aches.
- Weakened Immune System: With digestion on hold, gut health suffers, potentially impacting the body's ability to fight off illness.

- Sleep Disturbances: The constant state of "high alert" associated with chronic stress can make restful sleep difficult.

- Mood Swings and Weight Gain: Cortisol's influence can contribute to irritability, anxiety, increased appetite, and potential weight gain.

- Chronic Disease Risk: Over time, chronic stress can elevate the risk of health problems like heart disease, diabetes, and others.

By understanding the body's stress response, we can take steps to manage stress effectively and promote overall well-being.

Chronic Stress: Hijacks Mind and Actions

Chronic stress is like a thief in the brain, stealing your ability to function at your best. It primarily targets two key areas:

1. Frontal Lobe (Planning & Focus): Imagine your brain's control center – the prefrontal cortex. This area is responsible for setting goals, planning, organizing, prioritizing, and regulating emotions. Unfortunately, during

stress, this center gets sidelined. It's like putting your phone on airplane mode – essential functions become inaccessible.

2. Hippocampus (Memory Central): This is where memories are created and stored. Stress, with its surge of hormones, acts like a shrink ray on the hippocampus, making it harder to form new memories and impacting recall of existing ones.

These stolen brain functions translate to real-world struggles, like:

- Lose Focus: Simple tasks feel overwhelming, and concentration becomes a battle.
- Make Poor Decisions: Without clear thinking and planning, impulsive choices become more likely.
- Experience Emotional Rollercoaster: With the prefrontal cortex offline, managing emotions becomes a challenge, leading to irritability, mood swings, and difficulty regulating feelings.

The good news? There's a way out. Being "Active" – through exercise, stress-reduction techniques, or simply taking breaks – can help combat the negative effects of stress and restore balance to your brain. The next section will explore how yoga practices can help you combat stress and its negative impacts, promoting a healthier and happier you!

From Stress to Harmony

Yoga: The Antidote to Chronic Stress and Beyond

Sage Patanjali says,*"Dukkhanu sayee dweshaha"*- pain leads to anger, aversion.

Chronic stress, as we've seen, wreaks havoc on both mind and body. It manifests not only in emotional turmoil and behavioral changes, but also in physical ailments – a condition known as psychosomatic illness. In yogic philosophy, "Adhi" (the disturbed mind) is the root cause, and "Vyadhi" (the physical disease) is the outward symptom.

This is where yoga steps in as a powerful tool for managing chronic stress effectively. Here's why yoga is uniquely positioned to combat stress and its effects:

1. Holistic Approach: Yoga addresses both the psychological and physical aspects of stress, yoga creates a synergy between the two.

2. Restoring Balance: As its name suggests, *"Samatvam Yoga Uchyateh"* - Yoga is the union that brings balance, aims to restore equilibrium to the body's various systems, particularly the psycho-neuro-immuno-endocrine axis. This intricate network, encompassing the nervous, immune, and hormonal systems, plays a crucial role in stress response. By promoting balance within this axis, yoga fosters overall well-being.

3. Antioxidant Powerhouse: A yogic lifestyle, incorporating mindful movement, breath work, and a nourishing diet, relaxations techniques provides your body with a potent defense against free radicals – harmful molecules that contribute to stress-induced damage. This counteracts the negative effects of chronic stress and promotes healing.

4. Breath and Movement Synergy: Practicing the Yama -the restrains and Niyamas-the observances, integrating yoga postures (asana) with conscious breathing (pranayama) creates a powerful synergy.

This not only improves flexibility and strength but also promotes mental clarity and emotional regulation, leading to psychosomatic harmony.

By incorporating yogic practices into your life, you can effectively manage chronic stress, prevent the onset of stress-related illnesses, and cultivate a sense of well-being that extends far beyond the physical realm.

Note: Before practicing any yoga pose or techniques, it's important to be aware of any potential contraindications. Always ideal to practice under able guidance of a qualified yoga instructor.

The Magic of Yoga

A Practice for Holistic Healing: Ever felt the tension drain away as you settle into a comfortable position? Imagine this: you close your eyes in Vajrasana (Diamond Pose), feeling your breath whoosh in and out. Notice the rise and fall of your abdomen, the steady beat of your heart. As you inhale, raise your arms high, feeling a surge of energy flow through them. Stretch your chest, open your ribcage, and visualize clean air filling your lungs. Feel the blood pool in your core, a warm center of strength. Now, exhale and gently bend forward from the waist, a wave of blood rushing to your head as your spine lengthens. Arms outstretched, eyes closed, your mind turns inward (Pratyahara), worries melt away with each breath. Stay there for a few breaths. Relax, feel the stillness. Now, inhaling, slowly raise your head and torso, feel renewed energy flow to your lower body. Tell me, how do you feel now?

By focusing on your breath and body, the chatter in your mind quiets, replaced by a deep sense of calm. This is the magic of yoga – each pose, practiced with awareness, unlocks a pathway to holistic healing. It's not just about stretching or fancy postures; it's about connecting with yourself, reducing stress, and creating space for true well-being.

Yoga takes a holistic approach. It addresses the physical, mental, and emotional aspects of your well-being. This comprehensive approach is key to treating psychosomatic conditions, as it tackles the root causes of your symptoms, not just the surface-level issues.

Yoga is more than just stretching and fancy poses. It's a journey of self-discovery that unlocks the door to profound healing, stress reduction, and overall well-being. But how does it achieve this magic? The answer lies in the ancient wisdom of the Pancha Koshas, a concept from the Taittiriya Upanishad.

Healing Through the Koshas

Yoga Practices for Each Layer: Imagine your existence as a tapestry woven with five layers, each more subtle than the last. These are the Pancha Koshas:

1. *Annamaya Kosha (The Food Sheath):* This is your physical body, the one you can see and touch. It's the foundation, built from the five elements – earth, water, fire, air, and space. Yoga postures (asana) and cleansing practices (shat karma) can help detoxify your gross body, improve digestion, and boost metabolism, allowing for better nutrient absorption. Following a balanced diet based on your Ayurveda body type (Prakruti) further nourishes your body and mind, preparing it for seasonal changes too.

2. *Pranamaya Kosha (The Vital Energy Sheath):* Think of this as your energy body,

a network of life force (prana) flowing through channels (nadis) and swirling in energy centers (chakras). Breath acts as the bridge between the (physical) annamaya and manomaya, influencing both. *"Chale vateh chaleh chittam nischaleh nischalam bhavet"*|| Hatha yoga pradipika 2.2||As the wind moves, so does the mind. When the mind is still, so is the breath. Pranayama (breathing exercises) like Anulom Vilom cleanse these channels, promoting a healthy flow of energy. Other techniques like Bhramari pranayama (Bee Breath) soothe the mind, while mudras (hand gestures) like Gyan mudra and Pran mudra help channel energy effectively. Yogic breathing teaches you to respond thoughtfully, rather than reacting impulsively. It also supports better functioning of the digestive and nervous systems. Bandhas (body locks) stimulate nerve plexuses, hormone secretion, etc., while mudras act as seals regulating prana. It's important to practice these techniques under the guidance of a qualified teacher.

3. *Manomaya Kosha (The Mental Sheath)*:
   This is the realm of your emotions, thoughts, and perceptions. It's where your unique perspective shapes your experiences. The instability of this sheath can lead you astray and cause sorrow. Here, practices like mantra japa (chanting), knowledge acquisition, concentration (dharana), and dedicated practice (sadhana) can help bring stability. The sound "AUM" is a powerful mantra with profound effects.

4. *Vijnanamaya Kosha (The Wisdom Sheath)*: Delving deeper, we find the Vijnanamaya Kosha, the seat of your intellect, discrimination, and sense of self. This is where knowledge and understanding reside. This sheath influences hormone and enzyme secretion at various chakra points. Practices like meditation (dhyana), yogic sleep (yoga nidra), self-control, and self-study (swadhyaya) can cultivate wisdom. Studying scriptures and spending time with wise people also contribute to nurturing this layer.

5. *Anandamaya Kosha (The Bliss Sheath)*:
    Deep within lies the Anandamaya Kosha, the
    sheath of pure joy and bliss. It's the source of
    our deepest desires for connection and
    peace. Understanding your genes can offer
    insights into this Kosha. Practices like
    meditation (dhyana) focused on the
    Vishuddhi (throat), Agna (third eye), and
    Muladhara (root) chakras can help cultivate
    this blissful state.

Healing from the Inside Out
Modern Science Meets Ancient Wisdom

Stress – it's a constant companion in our fast-paced world. But what exactly happens when we're stressed? Science tells us chronic stress can disrupt the brain's ability to learn and adapt (neurogenesis and plasticity), and even damage brain cells (neurotoxicity).

One culprit behind this is perseverative cognition (PC). Imagine dwelling on stressful events, replaying them in your mind ("what-ifs," "should-haves"). This constant mental churning keeps your body in a heightened state of stress, even when the original stressor is gone.

Conclusion

The Power of Inner Peace: The research presented here paints a clear picture. Uncontrolled rumination on stress (perseverative cognition) is a major culprit behind many physical ailments. This highlights a crucial takeaway – managing our internal world might be even more important than trying to control every external stressor.

By learning to quiet the mind and break free from negative thought patterns, we empower ourselves to build resilience against stress and promote overall well-being. (Satyapriya, 2009).

The good news? Studies suggest tools to combat stress:

- Lifestyle changes: Practices like yoga and meditation can improve brain function and reduce stress response.
- Moderate exercise: Even a brisk walk can significantly lower stress levels.

- Social connections: Strong social networks act as a buffer against stress.

- Medication: In some cases, medication can be helpful.

We have understood the Upanishads, a collection of sacred texts, describing the human experience through five layers or "koshas." Classical yoga texts view stress as an imbalance within these koshas. Now, let's explore ancient wisdom's perspective on stress.

Aligning With the Bhagavad Gita

Overcoming Negative Patterns: The Bhagavad Gita, a revered scripture, highlights the mind-body connection. When Thought arises or challenges, our minds dwell on them repeatedly. This dwelling can turn into attachment, then escalate into desire, and even anger. These strong emotions create a ripple effect, impacting our inner world.

Imagine a calm lake reflecting the sky. Now, imagine throwing a pebble in the water. The surface becomes agitated, just like our minds become disturbed by strong emotions.

The yogic texts suggest that mastering these emotions is key to mental well-being. If we can't control them, they can lead to confusion, memory lapses, and even poor judgment.

It states that, "When the mind dwells on desires, desires lead to anger. Anger leads to delusion. Delusion leads to loss of memory. Loss of memory leads to destruction." (Bhagavad Gita 2.62-63) Therefore, dwelling on desires leads to anger, and anger clouds judgment, ultimately leading to our downfall. This aligns with the concept of the koshas. When the "thought sheath" (Manomaya Kosha) is troubled by endless thoughts, it disrupts the "energy sheath" (Pranamaya Kosha), leading to imbalances and ultimately, physical ailments (Annamaya Kosha).

The Takeaway

A Powerful Synthesis: Modern science and ancient wisdom offer a powerful combination for managing stress. By incorporating practices like yoga and meditation (modern) alongside self-reflection and building social connections (ancient), we can effectively combat stress and cultivate overall well-being. In essence, this approach allows us to leverage the benefits of technology and the profound knowledge of our scriptures.

By addressing each Kosha through various yoga practices, you can achieve balance from the inside out. Yoga activates the body's relaxation response, restoring normalcy to all systems, particularly the psycho-neuro-immuno-endocrine axis (which governs stress response, immunity, and hormone regulation). Combined with a balanced diet, yoga:

- Boosts antioxidants to fight free radicals (harmful molecules) caused by stress.
- Fuels your body with vital nutrients for healing and renewal.
- Integrates body movements with breath, creating psychosomatic harmony (balance between mind and body).

Yoga empowers you to heal not just physically but also mentally and emotionally. It's a journey of self-discovery, a path toward a healthier, happier you. Are you ready to begin?

Yoga's Path to Peace: Understanding the Philosophy

The research highlights the importance of managing our internal world to combat stress. Yoga offers a powerful toolkit to achieve this, drawing on ancient concepts like the five koshas (layers of our being) and pratiprasava (involution process).

Sage Patanjali, the father of yoga, believed suffering can be avoided, even before it arises. The yoga sutra, *"Heyam dukham anagatam"* which translates to "The Pain Which Is Yet to Come Is to Be Avoided." This philosophy forms the foundation of yoga's approach to de-stress.

Key concepts and practices Patanjali proposed:

1. Heya: The suffering- here in this case refers to Stress. State of mind can be equated to agitated (kshipta) state.

2. Heyahetu: The cause of suffering, here it refers to the Stressors. These are the root causes of stress, like negative thoughts (kleshas) such as clinging to identity (asmita).

3. Hana: It refers to the desired outcome which is Peaceful State of mind; a mind free from suffering and stress.

4. Hanopaya: It refers to the ways to achieve the desired outcome, tools for Peace. These are the practices of yoga, particularly the Eight Limbs of Yoga (Ashtanga Yoga), which help us achieve inner peace, providing a holistic approach to stress management.

Sage Patanjali, the great psychologist, understood the fluctuations of the mind and suggested various levels of practices. He recommended Ashtanga Yoga for beginners, Kriya Yoga for intermediate practitioners, and for the highest level of practitioners, Abhyasa (consistent practice) and Vairagya (dispassion).

Ashtanga Yoga

A Multi-Limbed Approach to De-Stress

In the context of stress, one might not be able to immediately start with advanced practices but can begin slowly and with ease.

Here are some key practices to incorporate:

Ashtanga yoga: 8 limbs of yoga namely; Yama (abstinences), Niyama (observances), Asana (yoga postures), Pranayama (breath control), Pratyahara (withdrawal of the senses), Dharana (concentration), Dhyana (meditation) and Samadhi (absorption).

Yama & Niyama:

"Yoga emphasizes Yama and Niyama—the dos and don'ts. Yama: Ethical guidelines for behavior towards others; Niyama: Personal observances for self-discipline.

They are to be practiced with respect to others and oneself in every thought, word, and deed. For example, Santosh, the Niyama, guides us to be satisfied and content with what we have. It bestows "anuttama sukha labhaha"—immense happiness, says Sage Patanjali.

Asana: We have seen with the example of Vajrasana how you can retain composure and be in the present moment. In Asana practice, we need to focus on maintaining the posture for a certain period of time without discomfort for maximum benefits and experience. "Tato dwandva anabhighataha"|| After mastering the pose, the sadhak (practitioner) is unperturbed by the dualities of life, says Sage Patanjali.

Pranayama: We have seen the power of Pranayama in cleansing the pathways and bringing about balance in the sympathetic and parasympathetic nervous systems. Yoga Guru Iyengar has said, "Pranayama is like the hub of yoga, where the individual and the cosmic meet." By continuous practice of Pranayama, "tatah ksheeyateh prakaasa avaranam," || 2.52|| says sage Patanjali. From Pranayama practice, the cover that obscures light (the veil) is destroyed, and prepares the mind for concentration- dharana.

Pratyahara: Pratyahara, the yogic practice of turning the mind to introspection by voluntarily shutting out distractions provided by the senses, helps us turn inward, creating a calm, peaceful environment and a satvic (balanced) mind.

Meditation (Dhyana): Meditation, the cornerstone of yoga, offers a wealth of benefits.

- Reduced Stress and Anxiety: Meditation helps calm the mind and reduce stress hormones, leading to a more peaceful state.

- Promotes Emotional Health: By fostering self-awareness, meditation allows you to observe and manage your emotions more effectively.

- Enhances Self-Awareness: Meditation cultivates a deeper understanding of your thoughts, feelings, and patterns.

- Lengthens Attention Span: Regular meditation practice can improve your ability to focus and concentrate.

- May Reduce Age-Related Memory Loss: Some research suggests meditation may help preserve cognitive function as we age.

- Cultivates Kindness: Meditation practices often cultivate compassion and a sense of well-being, which can extend to others.

- May Help Fight Addictions: Meditation can be a valuable tool for managing cravings and increasing self-control.

- Improves Sleep: A calm mind promotes better sleep quality.

* Helps Control Pain Perception: Meditation can alter your perception of pain, making it more manageable.

By clearing away mental clutter and promoting relaxation, meditation can significantly reduce stress. While a wealth of research supports its benefits, some experts believe further studies are needed to fully understand the impact of different meditation practices on specific conditions. Regardless, it's important to find a qualified teacher or reliable resources to guide you in establishing a safe and effective meditation practice.

Yoga to De-stress: A Beginner's Guide

This guide offers a gentle introduction to some key practices that can help you manage stress and find inner peace. Remember, yoga is a journey, not a destination, so be patient and kind to yourself.

Getting Started

Before diving in, remember these tips:

* Listen to your body: Start slow and gradually increase the difficulty as you get more comfortable.

- Focus on your breath: Deep, rhythmic breathing throughout your practice is key to relaxation.
- Find a quiet space: Create a calm and distraction-free environment for your practice.
- Be consistent: Regular practice is essential to experience the long-term benefits of yoga.

Simple yet Effective

Quick De-Stress daily routine: This short routine combines gentle stretches, relaxation poses, and breathing exercises – perfect for beginners!

Firstly gentle warm up. Next, remember those sticky note reminders, "TAKE A DEEP BREATH IN AND RELAX" that we shared? Let's put them into practice! These simple yet powerful techniques can be incorporated into your daily life to combat stress.

1. Deep Breathing and Relaxation: Inhale deeply, filling your lungs with air. Hold for a few seconds, then exhale slowly. Repeat this process several times, focusing on the sensation of your breath.

2. Body Scan and Tension Release: Gently tighten your entire body, holding the tension for a few seconds. Slowly release the tension, allowing your muscles to relax. Pay attention to any areas of particular tension and focus on releasing them. Practice this technique upon waking, throughout the day, before sleep, or whenever you feel stressed.

3. Targeted Tension Relief:

> Eyes: Gently roll your eyes in circles, then blink rapidly to release tension.

> Shoulders: Shrug your shoulders up towards your ears, hold, and then release.

> Jaw: Open and close your mouth slowly, then gently massage your jaw muscles.

"These exercises may seem simple, but their impact on reducing stress and improving overall well-being is significant. Remember, consistency is key. Incorporate these practices into your daily routine for optimal results."

4. Om Chanting: Seek a peaceful environment free from distractions.

- Sit in a meditative pose like Sukhasana (Easy Pose) or Padmasana (Lotus Pose). Ensure your spine is straight and your body feels grounded.
- Focusing on the breath, take a few deep breaths to calm your mind and body.
- Gently begin to chant the sound of "A-U-M," prolonging each sound. Feel the vibration resonate through your body.
- Continue chanting for a minimum of 21 repetitions, focusing on the sound and its effect on your mind and body.
- After completing the chants, sit in silence for a few moments, observing the subtle changes within yourself.
- Regular practice of Om chanting can lead to profound benefits.

Deep Relaxation (Shavasana):
- Lie comfortably on your back with arms at your sides and palms facing up. Close your eyes and focus on your breath.
- Imagine releasing tension with each exhale.

- Stay in this state for 10-15 minutes. Shavasana promotes relaxation, reduces stress, and calms the nervous system.

Do More with Yoga Nidra:

- Yoga Nidra, also known as yogic sleep, is a powerful relaxation technique. It's like guided meditation while lying down. Here's a simplified explanation of the stages:

- Get Comfortable: Lie down in a relaxing position. Close your eyes and take deep breaths.

- Body Scan: Imagine traveling through your body, noticing any sensations without judgment.

- Focus on Breath: Simply observe your natural breathing rhythm.

- Opposites Exploration: Imagine pairs of opposite sensations like heaviness and lightness in different parts of your body.

- Visualization: Use calming imagery – a peaceful meadow or receiving positive energy.

- Intention Repetition: Silently repeat your chosen goal or positive affirmation.

- Gently Waking Up: The guide will slowly bring you back to full awareness.
- Integration (Optional): Reflect on your experience and carry the positive feelings into your day.

Benefits of Yoga Nidra:

- Reduced stress
- Improved sleep
- Increased self-awareness
- Emotional balance
- Enhanced creativity
- Deep relaxation and inner peace

Important Note: While you can find online resources for Yoga Nidra, it's best to learn from a qualified teacher who can guide you through the stages safely. Remember, yoga is a practice for everyone. With these beginner-friendly tips and the power of Yoga Nidra, you can embark on a journey to de-stress, to rejuvenate and inner peace.

Kriya Yoga is a powerful yogic practice that combines three key elements: Tapas, Swadhyaya and Eswar pranidhan.

1. **Tapas** (Self-Discipline): Tapas, the first pillar of Kriya Yoga, is about self-discipline. It's about pushing yourself gently outside your comfort zone to cultivate inner strength and purification.

   Here are some examples applied to different aspects of life (thought, word and deed):

   - *Bodily Tapas (Physical Discipline): For e.g.* Following a regular yoga practice even if you're new, committing to practicing yoga a few times a week is tapas. As you progress, you can gradually increase the duration or difficulty of your practice.

   - Maintaining good posture: Throughout the day, consciously remind yourself to sit up straight and avoid slouching. This small act of awareness strengthens your core and improves your overall well-being.

   - Eating moderately and mindfully: Instead of mindless snacking, choose healthy foods and eat until you're comfortably satisfied. This promotes healthy digestion and reduces cravings.

- ➢ *Speech Tapas (Disciplined Speech):* Practicing mindful communication: Think before you speak. Avoid gossip, negativity, or harsh words. Choose to speak kindly and truthfully.
- ➢ Limiting excessive talking: Be mindful of how much you talk, especially in social settings. Sometimes, listening actively is more important than speaking constantly.
- ➢ Practicing silence: Set aside some time each day for quiet reflection. This could involve meditation, spending time in nature, or simply sitting in silence.
- ➢ **Mental Tapas** (Mental Discipline): Maintaining a positive focus: Make a conscious effort to focus on the positive aspects of your life, even during challenging times.

➢ Cultivating gratitude: Take time each day to appreciate the good things in your life, big or small. This fosters a sense of contentment and reduces negativity.

➢ Limiting distractions: In today's digital world, it's easy to get overwhelmed by constant notifications and stimuli. Dedicate time for focused activities without distractions like your phone or social media.

Start small, celebrate your progress, and be patient with yourself. By consistently practicing self-discipline, you'll build inner strength, improve your focus, and cultivate a more peaceful state of mind.

2. **Swadhyaya** (Self-Study): This is about actively learning and understanding yourself. It involves introspection, studying yogic texts, and reflecting on your experiences.

   Think of it like exploring a new city. You might use a map or guidebook, but you also explore side streets and discover hidden gems on your own. This exploration deepens your understanding of the city, just like self-study deepens your understanding of yourself.

3. **Ishwar Pranidhana** (Surrender to a Higher Power): This doesn't necessarily mean subscribing to a specific religion. It's about cultivating a sense of trust in something larger than yourself, whether it's nature, the universe, or a divine force.
Imagine a child completely trusting their parents to provide for them. Similarly, Ishwar Pranidhana allows you to let go of anxieties and worries, trusting that a higher power will guide you. This frees you to focus on your present actions and reduces stress.

By integrating these three elements, Kriya Yoga offers numerous benefits namely:

- *Cultivates Inner Peace*: Surrendering anxieties and focusing on self-discipline and self-knowledge promote calmness and emotional stability.

- *Reduces the Impact of Kleshas*: Kleshas are mental afflictions that cause suffering, such as anger, jealousy, or greed. Kriya Yoga helps weaken their hold on you.

- *Increases Confidence and Strength*: Tapas builds inner resilience, while Swadhyaya fosters self-awareness and self-acceptance. Kriya Yoga is a powerful tool for managing stress and achieving inner peace.

The sutra 2.28 of Yoga darshan by sage Patanjali explains, "*From the practice of the elements of ashtanga yoga comes the destruction of impurities; (therefrom)comes the shine of knowledge that stretches all the way to the domain of discernment.*"

Summary

These practices form a comprehensive system for managing stress and promoting health and peace. By starting with the basics and gradually advancing, one can achieve significant improvements in well-being and mental clarity.

 Consistency is key. By incorporating these practices regularly, you can gradually remove the "veil" that obscures your inner light and cultivate lasting peace, even before stress arises.

- ❖ *The Power of Positive Thinking:* Yoga emphasizes cultivating positive attitudes like kindness (Maitri), compassion (Karuna), joy for others' happiness (Mudita), and equanimity (Upeksha). This mental shift fosters a more peaceful and positive outlook. In the book psychology of serenity I have in detail discussed these four virtues for a peaceful state of mind.

- ❖ *Pratipaksha Bhavana*: Is a powerful yogic technique, involves cultivating opposite qualities to counteract negative thoughts and emotions that lead to suffering. When negativity arises, counter it with positive emotions. This practice helps break free from negative thought patterns. "Vitarka badhane pratipaksha bhavanam" (II Sutra 33) *"When improper thoughts trouble you, then take the opposite side."*

This practice is rooted in Patanjali's Yoga Sutras, specifically Sutra II.34, which states:

"Vitarka himsadayaha kurta karitanumodita lobha krodha mohapurvaka mrudu Madhya adhimatra dukhajnanantaphala iti pratipaksha bhavanam"

This sutra highlights that negative thoughts and actions lead to suffering, while cultivating opposite qualities brings happiness and peace. It emphasizes replacing negative thoughts with positive ones, replacing destructive actions with constructive ones, and replacing harmful emotions with beneficial ones.

Here's how you can incorporate Pratipaksha Bhavana into your daily life:

> ➢ Example 1: Replacing Anger with Compassion
>
> Situation: You feel a surge of anger towards someone who has wronged you.
>
> Negative Thought: "I'll never forgive them. They deserve to be punished."
>
> Pratipaksha Bhavana: "I understand that they may be going through a difficult time. I choose to extend compassion and understanding towards them."

Action: Instead of reacting in anger, you calmly approach the person and try to understand their perspective.

➢ Example 2: Replacing Anxiety with Mindfulness

Situation: You're feeling anxious about an upcoming presentation.

Negative Thought: "I'm going to mess up. Everyone will judge me."

Pratipaksha Bhavana: "I've prepared well for this presentation. I'll focus on the present moment and deliver my message with clarity and confidence."

Action: Instead of letting anxiety consume you, you practice deep breathing exercises and focus on the present moment.

➢ Example 3: Replacing Greed with Contentment

Situation: You're constantly comparing yourself to others and feeling dissatisfied with your possessions.

Negative Thought: "I need more to be happy. I'll never have enough."

Pratipaksha Bhavana: "I am grateful for the abundance in my life. I choose to focus on the positive aspects of what I have rather than dwelling on what I lack."

Action: Instead of chasing material possessions, you focus on cultivating inner contentment and appreciating the simple joys in life.

- ➤ Recognize the presence of envy and its potential to cause suffering.
- ➤ Shift your focus to the things you're grateful for in your own life.
- ➤ Celebrate the achievements of others without feeling diminished.
- ➤ Channel your energy into pursuing your own aspirations with determination.

Remember, it requires consistent effort and patience. With regular practice, you can gradually transform your negative thought patterns and cultivate a more peaceful and fulfilling life.

Sakshi Bhava, meaning "witness state" in Sanskrit, goes beyond simply being aware. It's about cultivating a deep awareness of yourself, both internally and externally. Imagine yourself as a silent observer, a Sakshi, completely present in the moment. You're not lost in the sights, sounds, smells, or the constant chatter of your mind. This centered state allows you to observe your thoughts and emotions without judgment, preventing them from controlling your reactions.

Here's an example: Have you ever felt overwhelmed by anger or frustration in a situation? Sakshi Bhava offers a practical approach. When you encounter a trigger, take a deep breath. This pause creates space between the situation and your reaction. Now, become the observer. Imagine your mind as a movie screen, and your thoughts and emotions as the images playing out. You, the Sakshi, are simply watching the show. Label your thoughts – are you feeling angry, frustrated, or anxious? By labeling them, you create a separation and prevent them from taking over. As you observe, they lose power over you. Finally, let go of judgment. Don't judge yourself or your thoughts. Simply observe them as if they were clouds passing by in the sky.

Benefits of Sakshi Bhava:

- Increased self-awareness: By observing your thoughts and actions, you gain a deeper understanding of yourself.

- Reduced emotional reactivity: You learn to detach from your emotions, allowing for calmer responses.

- Enhanced mental clarity: Detaching from the constant mental chatter leads to greater clarity, focus and productivity.

- Improved decision-making: With clear thinking, you can make more thoughtful choices.

- Promotes inner peace: By observing your emotions without judgment, you experience greater peace and well-being.

Remember: Abhyas i.e. Practice. Sakshi Bhava is a practice, and like any skill, it takes time and effort. Start by incorporating short periods of observation throughout your day. With consistent practice, you'll cultivate a witnessing attitude that empowers you to navigate life's situations with greater awareness and peace.

Sage Patanjali says, Abhyasa

Cultivating Stillness with Patience and Respect: In the Yoga Sutras, Sage Patanjali emphasizes the importance of Abhyasa, which translates to "practice" or "effort." It's about cultivating a state of stillness and presence with dedication and respect.
Understanding the Sutra:
The sutra, "sa tu dirgha kala nairantarya satkara sevito drudha bhumihi", i.e. "This becomes (The practice) firmly established in you when you attend to it for a long time, without interruption and with devotion."
- Patanjali Yoga Sutra ||1.14||
Example: Learning an Instrument
Imagine learning an instrument like the piano. Playing a few notes here and there won't make you a master. True mastery comes from practicing regularly for a long time, with dedication and a respect for the instrument and the art form. Similarly, Abhyasa cultivates stillness in the mind, but it takes consistent effort and respect for the

practice. Be patient with yourself, celebrate your progress, and approach your practice with respect and dedication. Over time, you'll cultivate a state of stillness that becomes an anchor in your life.

By incorporating these practices, you can address the root cause of stress within your mind and cultivate a sense of inner peace. Remember, yoga is a journey, not a destination. Start slowly, find a practice that resonates with you, and be patient with yourself. You'll be well on your way to managing stress and living a happier, healthier life.

Cultivating Inner Peace: Yogic Lifestyle Habits

The ancient wisdom of yoga emphasizes the connection between our daily habits and inner peace. Here's how you can integrate yogic principles into your life for a more balanced and stress-free existence:

- *Nourish Your Body and Mind:* Eat right. Choose a wholesome, satvic diet that fuels your body and mind. Avoid processed foods and excessive sugar that can drain your energy. Satvic foods are pure, light, and nourishing – as emphasized in Sri Bhagavad Gita. These foods support mental clarity, energy levels, and overall health.

- *Create a Supportive Environment*: Surround yourself with positive influences and declutter your living space. A clean and organized environment can contribute to a calmer mind.

- *Prioritize Your Well-Being*: Manage your time effectively. Respect your body's natural rhythms. Avoid overloading your schedule and prioritize activities that contribute to your well-being. Pacing yourself allows you to manage stress and function at your best.

- *Choose Your Company Wisely*: Negative influences can significantly impact your mood and stress levels. Surround yourself with positive and supportive individuals who uplift and motivate you.

- *Tame Your Desires and Cultivate Peace*: Unmanaged desires can be a major source of stress. Learn to control impulsive urges and cultivate healthy thought patterns. Practice gratitude for what you have instead of dwelling on what you lack.

- *Align Your Thoughts, Words, and Actions*: As the saying goes, "Yat bhavam tat bhavati" – you become what you think. Positive thoughts lead to positive actions and ultimately, a more peaceful life. Yoga philosophy emphasizes moderation and living with integrity (Aachar, Vichar, Vyavahara) – aligning your thoughts, words, and actions.

"Yukta hara vihaarasya yukta chestasya karmasu |
Yukta svapnanavabhodasya yogo bhavati dukhaha ||"
Sri Krishna says, "He who is moderate in food, activity, entertainment, sleep and wakefulness attains yoga which destroys suffering".
Remember these healthy habits are like building blocks for inner peace. By incorporating them into

your daily life, you can create a foundation for greater well-being and a more fulfilling existence.

Ancient Wisdom, Modern Solutions: Yoga's Diverse Approaches

The beauty of yoga lies in its diverse approaches to well-being. Here's a glimpse into some key yogic texts and their focus. The Hatha Yoga Pradipika focuses on balancing the body's physical and mental energies through yogic practices and leading to Raja yoga. The Yoga Sutras of Patanjali outline practices like ashtanga yoga, pratipaksha bhavana, inculcating virtues like maitri, karuna, etc for mental well-being. Meanwhile, Sri Bhagavad Gita teaches the importance of detachment from outcomes to maintain inner peace, even in challenging situations. In Bhagavad Gita, devotion and surrenderance is emphasized as a powerful tool for managing stress and finding inner peace. The Vedas and Upanishads emphasize achieving inner peace and recognizing the interconnectedness of all things. Finally, the Yoga Vashishtha as well delves into transcending mental limitations and achieving a higher state of consciousness.

By integrating the teachings from these various sources and practicing yoga regularly, you can cultivate resilience, inner peace, and a holistic approach to well-being that benefits your mind, body, and spirit. Sage Patanjali said, "From the practice of the elements of yoga comes the destruction of impurities; [therefrom] comes the shine of knowledge that stretches all the way to the domain of discernment." This highlights the transformative power of yoga practices.

We've explored the wisdom of yoga for managing stress, from its ancient texts to practical lifestyle tips. To truly benefit from these practices, it's essential to practice under the guidance of a knowledgeable yoga guru. The practices shared in this book are designed to help you navigate modern stress with timeless wisdom. Sri Krishna Pattabhi Jois said,"Yoga is 99% practice and 1% theory."

I quote, "When mind is quiet, the intellect becomes sharper, emotions become positive and lighter & our behavior becomes much more palatable."

Psychosomatic disorders like Stress can thus be treated through practice of regular yoga regime and with an attitude of giving your best and not worry of the results it bears. For; when one is focused and does their best, are bound to get good results even otherwise must as well develop an attitude of acceptance for healthy state of living.

This positive transformation, strength, wisdom is definitely possible through yoga abhyas. "HEYAM DUKHAM ANAGATAM". So, are you ready to embark on a journey of self-discovery and inner peace through the ancient practices of yoga?

Brahmabindu Upanishad says:-

Manaeve manushyaanaam Kaaranam bandhamokshayoh|

Bandhaaya vishayaasaktam muktyai nirvishayam smrutam||

"As the mind, so the man; bondage or liberation are in our own mind."

CHAPTER 6

Connecting Through Yoga

Rishi turned the last page of the booklet with a satisfied sigh. He glanced at the clock, surprised to see an hour had flown by. "Wow," he thought, "time just melted away while I was reading this!"

Excited to share his newfound knowledge, Rishi opened his community yoga group chat and typed:

"Hey everyone! Just finished reading the amazing booklet Yogi Seshi shared – so much incredible information! I can't believe how quickly I devoured it all. Now I'm feeling a little overwhelmed, but in the best way possible! So many beautiful practices, so much valuable knowledge! Where do I even begin? How do I implement all of this into my life?"#YogaNewbie #StressedButHopeful

Within seconds, replies started pouring in:

Aditi: "Ha-ha, Rishi, welcome to the wonderful world of yoga! It can be overwhelming at first, but don't worry. We've all been there! The beauty is you can start small. What resonated with you most while reading?"

Ravi: "Totally agree, Aditi! Maybe pick one practice that really piqued your interest, Rishi. Like meditation, or maybe some breathing exercises. Start there and build gradually. Consistency is key!"

Sarah: "There are also some great yoga guru who take regular sessions, Rishi! They can guide you through different practices and routines. Let me know if you'd like some recommendations."

Rishi smiled, feeling a wave of gratitude wash over him. "This community is amazing!" he typed. "Thanks everyone for the advice. I think I'll start with some basic breathing exercises – that calming technique really caught my eye. And Sarah, I'd love those gurukul recommendations if you have a moment!"

Yogi Seshi: (Joining the conversation) "Excellent choices, Rishi! Remember, yoga is a journey, not a destination and Moderation is the key. Enjoy the process, and don't hesitate to ask questions along the way. This community is here to support you on your yoga journey! Namaste. "

Rishi felt a surge of motivation. With the support of his community and Yogi Seshi's wisdom, he was ready to embark on his own personal yoga journey, one step (or breath) at a time.

Let's empower ourselves and each other to cultivate a healthier, more balanced lifestyle through the transformative practice of yoga.

May We Radiate Love & Light

||Sarve Jana Sukhinobhavantu ||

ACKNOWLEDGEMENT

I extend my sincere gratitude to my esteemed yoga gurus for their invaluable guidance and inspiration. Their teachings have been the cornerstone of my journey. I am deeply indebted to my family and friends for their unwavering support and encouragement. Their belief in me has been a constant source of motivation.

I would like to express my heartfelt appreciation to Dr. Manjunath Sir for conceptualizing the program that accelerated my growth. His mentorship has been instrumental in shaping my skills and aspirations. I am truly grateful to Som Bathla Sir for his invaluable guidance in refining my writing and communication abilities. His expertise has been instrumental in effectively conveying the essence of this work.

I acknowledge the wealth of knowledge shared on online platforms, which significantly enriched my understanding. Thank you.

Reference

Rajesh SK, Ilavarasu JV, Srinivasan TM, Nagendra HR. Stress and its Expression According to Contemporary Science and Ancient Indian Wisdom: Perseverative Cognition and the Pañca kośas. Mens Sana Monogr. 2014 Jan;12(1):139-52. doi: 10.4103/0973-1229.130323. PMID: 24891803; PMCID: PMC4037893.

Ornish D, Scherwitz LW, Billings JH, et al. Intensive Lifestyle Changes for Reversal of Coronary Heart Disease. *JAMA*. 1998;280(23):2001–2007. doi:10.1001/jama.280.23.2001